Dawna

Laugh, Love and Live faithfully

Mae Duane

Endorsements

Mrs. Ford sends you her best wishes. She enjoyed reading the excerpts that you sent and knows that, just by writing the book, you have not only helped yourself but will surely help many others.

Jan Hart, Personal Assistant to Betty Ford

Alpha Chick *is Mal Duane's inspirational memoir for women who want the rewarding, fulfilling and happy life they've always dreamed about but didn't know how to achieve. Listen to your intuition, follow Mal's well-defined, doable steps, and you'll be led into the light of happiness and success!*

Lynn A. Robinson, Author
LISTEN: Trusting Your Inner Voice in Times of Crisis

At the time I needed it the most, Alpha Chick *appeared in my life. Every word Mal wrote gave me encouragement, peace of mind, increased faith and a deepened belief that I can make it through anything . . . and experience more blessings and miracles than ever before. Thank you, Mal, for sharing your story and offering such inspiration for women!*

Christine Kloser, Award-Winning Author
The Freedom Formula: How to Put Soul into Your Business and Money in Your Bank

The tried and true principles in Mal Duane's Alpha Chick *can help women from all walks of life achieve success, happiness and an overall positive mental transformation. Whether a woman has experienced a broken heart, has an addictive personality, or just needs to find a way to cultivate positive change in her life, the 5 steps in the Alpha Chick Process will put her on the road to meeting all of life's challenges with a full heart and a confident attitude.*

Melysha J. Acharya, Author
The Breakup Workbook: A Common Sense Guide to Getting Over Your Ex

Mal Duane's book . . . gives us an insightful, practical and loving guide to shift our life story from one of pain and suffering to one of power and possibility. All women are recovering from something, whether it is a failed marriage, the loss of a loved one, an unexpected illness, a career change or an addiction. Alpha Chick *shows us how to accept and transform our painful life experiences and losses, into divine opportunities for personal growth and healing. This book is for any women in the midst of a life transition that longs for a renewed sense of hope, strength and a brighter perspective on her current situation.*
Michele Wahlder, MS, LPC,
Founder, Life Possibilities and Author
Alphatudes: The Alphabet of Gratitude

Mal Duane, in her inspiring book, Alpha Chick, *takes the reader on a spell binding journey of her life. She climbs emotional hills, descends into behavioral valleys and through it all, maintains her ability to face life fairly and squarely. Her painful journey into and out of active alcoholism (both her own and her family of origin) is a story that many women will recognize as similar to their experience. Her ability to understand the recovery process and put into words a clear and available formula for recovery can be understood and accepted. As Mal describes recovery, the reader can fully understand and accept the five steps of Faith for change and healing. Her plan of moving from pain to power is a valuable guidepost and support for any woman who wants to grow and find strength, hope and power.*

   She supports the philosophy that each of us grows in our own recovery as we help others face their hills and valleys and continue the path toward complete healing.
Sharon Wegscheider-Cruse, Best Selling Author
Learning to Love Yourself, **Family Therapist, Founding Chairperson of National Association for Children of Alcoholics and Founder of Onsite Workshops**

ALPHA CHICK

ALPHA CHICK

Five steps

for moving

from pain

to power

MAL DUANE

www.AlphaChick.com

Alpha Chick: Five Steps for Moving from Pain to Power

Copyright © 2012 Mal Duane

Published by:
Alpha Chick Press
256 Salem End Rd.
Framingham, MA 01702
www.AlphaChick.com

Publisher's Cataloging-In-Publication

Duane, Mal.
    Alpha chick : five steps for moving from pain to power / Mal Duane.
    - Framingham, MA : Alpha Chick Press, c2011.
        p. ; cm.
        ISBN: 978-0-9834129-0-8 (soft cover edition)
        ISBN: 978-0-9834129-1-5 (ebook edition)

    1. Self-help techniques. 2. Self-esteem in women. 3. Recovery
movement. 4. Achievement motivation in women. 5. Women--
Psychology.

HQ1206 .   D83 2011 2011907138
155.6/33--dc22   1106

Library of Congress Control Number: 201 1907138
ISBN:978-0-9834129-0-8

Printed in the United States of America

Book Design: Illumination Graphics
Editing: Barbara Doern Drew
Book Consultant: Ellen Reid

This book is dedicated to

Holly

My life was blessed with a shining star. The influence that Holly had on me and so many others can never be fully expressed with words. Her dedication and commitment to everything she undertook was highly inspirational. She taught me patience, grace, compassion, courage, and ultimately acceptance of what life offers. She was the guiding compass in my life.

Gratefully, my lessons continue. I hear Holly's voice in my meditations, inspiring me to be more and do more—her Golden Rule. Her essence was that of a true Alpha Chick, and her light will always shine brightly on all of us who knew her.

Two books in one to encourage and guide you to uncovering your own true magnificence

Like many women, Mal Duane endured some pretty rough times. An ugly duckling child, she found herself surrounded by viciously mean "friends" whose cruel criticisms destroyed virtually every vestige of Mal's self-esteem. Life at home became increasingly tense eventually pushing Mal to a complete disconnect from her parents. Later, despite having evolved into a striking beauty and successful model, genuine relationships eluded her and heartache and self-loathing were frequent companions. But in her late teens, Mal had found a coping solution: Alcohol.

By her mid 40s her life seemed all but over. She was spiraling downward, hopelessly out of control. Then a final heartbreak pushed her over the edge and she found herself looking death right in the eye. From the fires of that particular hell, Mal, Alpha Chick, emerged. She chose to shed her past and start living.

Alpha Chick is more than just Mal's road to happiness, success, and fulfillment. It is a model for any woman who dreams of those things.

The first part of the book is Mal's painfully honest story. Its purpose is to illustrate just how far off track Mal had been and to inspire you to be able to pick yourself up as Mal did, no matter how far off course your life has gone.

Inspiration, however, is rarely enough to carry you through. And that's the importance of the second part of the book. It presents Mal's practical plan for transforming pain to power and sets you firmly on the road to becoming an Alpha Chick. It grew out of her own recovery process and revealed itself during one of her daily meditations. Her epiphany was that the plan had five steps. And it did not surprise her that the foundation letter of each step spelled out a single significant word:

Focus
Acceptance and Attitude
Identification and Intention
Thoughts
Healing and Helping

The brilliance of this program is not that it shows you how to become a *Mal Duane* Alpha Chick. Its genius is that it clearly guides you to becoming your own unique brand of Alpha Chick. It sets you on your own road to being the ideal you; the sizzling, empowered woman you are meant to be.

Alpha Chick shows you how to recapture self-love, faith, and hope. It provides all you need to create a new vision and to achieve your new, exceptional life filled with passion, purpose and power.

Contents

Part One
From Innocence to Obsession to Transformation

Part Two
The Five Steps of the Alpha Chick Process

Acknowledgments

I am so grateful for the remarkable people who have supported and inspired me along my path to discovering my inner strength, peace, and purpose in life. Since our first meeting at the end of 2001, the greatest influence in my life has been my kind, intelligent, and loving husband, Michael Pearlman, aka "Dr. Delicious." Michael encouraged me to share the story of my alcoholism and the dysfunction it had created in my life. He believed I had a powerful message that would help other women. Michael, you have inspired me to take chances, to grow, to believe in myself, and to not be afraid to appreciate my imperfections, and, by doing so, to release them.

The chapter "Sweet Pea" provides a small glimpse of the most inspiring young woman I have ever known, my niece, Holly. She taught me what is really important in life: courage and perseverance. Although gravely ill, she spent her days caring about others and always trying to ensure that her illness did not intrude upon their lives. She never resisted or denied her condition; instead, she lived her life fully and courageously. As my grief subsided after she died and I was able to think about her life, her strength, and her determination, I knew I wanted to write a book that would honor her—a book to inspire and support women to help themselves and grow in strength. Holly's spirit gave me the energy to begin writing *Alpha Chick*, and she was with me as I wrote every page.

I am grateful to master coach and Science of Mind practitioner Siobhan Murphy for introducing me to the Science of Mind spiritual philosophy. Siobhan taught me the power of prayer and how to use the Law of Attraction. She also showed me how to exercise leadership from the heart. Her strong spiritual guidance, patience, and comforting and reassuring words during challenging times in my life have been invaluable.

After I had written the first draft of *Alpha Chick*, I shared the manuscript with my good friend and client Joan Fallon. Joan loved the message of the book and enthusiastically offered to help me arrange my thoughts more clearly on paper and assist me with editing the material. For eight months, we met weekly, recording our meetings and adding details to the book. Her suggestions were flawless and her insight into the purpose of the book most helpful.

For two years, my soul sister Ann Peckham listened daily as I talked about the challenges I faced while writing *Alpha Chick*. She always expressed her belief in me and my ability to write and finish the book. I was comforted by the knowledge that I could call her at any time, day or night, to hear words of encouragement and compassion.

In the summer of 2008, I experienced a medical emergency that required surgery, followed by complications for several months thereafter. My personal trainer and good friend Rhonda Skloff helped push me through the resulting fatigue and gradually brought me back to my previous level of strength. She also gave me inspiration to continue writing *Alpha Chick* during the times when I was discouraged by the physical challenges presented by my recovery. Now Rhonda shows me how to stay healthy.

Finally, thank you to Maggie Lichtenberg, my book coach, and to Barbara Doern Drew for putting her brilliant final edits on the book and allowing me to fully know the potential of *Alpha Chick*.

Foreword

Clearly, nearly everyone experiences some degree of assault to their self-esteem levels and has their own story to share about how it all transpired. Mal Duane is no different. You'll find her story in the pages that follow to be interesting, humorous, entertaining, tragically sad, and inspirational. In sharing her own personal triumph and transformation from low self-esteem, depression, failed relationships and the downward spiral of alcoholism to self-love, happiness, fulfillment, and contribution, Mal inspires us to see that we all share common characteristics that can rob us of our personal power and prevent us from living our dream lives if we allow them to do so. Her story of overcoming the challenges of her first four decades goes far beyond just entertaining us. Mal actually teaches us the very same principles she personally used to transform her own life to one of joy, abundance, rich relationships and fulfillment.

From realizing the value of living intentionally to making the law of attraction work in your life, Mal spells out in clear and compelling step by step fashion a remarkable formula for transforming any life that may be characterized by struggle, suffering, and the tragic consequences of low self-esteem to one of self-respect and positive expectation. Her action guide exercises allow readers to map the life-impacting principles she shares onto their daily lives with dramatic results.

I invite you to not just read but devour this book, take on the lessons and principles Mal shares and look for how each one can specifically enhance your life to be taken to the next level. As human beings, we are all inherently magnificent – although too many of us forget this fact all too often. Enjoy Mal's gift to champion your magnificence and decide now to give up your right to invalidate yourself or suffer any longer by thinking that all the good things that the world has to offer are for other people but not you. Step into your personal power, love yourself and others, contribute your gifts to the world, decide what it will be and live your life purpose and know that anything you can dream, you can achieve if you have the courage to do so.

– Dr. Joe Rubino

Founder, CenterForPersonalReinvention.com

A Note from Mal

Dear Sisters,

Are you sick and tired of waking up paralyzed by guilt or dread over past mistakes, fearful of how you will get through the day, and suffocating with anxiety over tomorrow? If the answer is yes, please know that I have a sense of how you feel because I have been in that very place myself. In fact, this is why I have written this book—to let you know that you are not alone and that there are other possibilities for you. While there are many books currently written about *getting* what you want, *Alpha Chick: Five steps for moving from pain to power* is about *becoming* the person you were meant to be—living a life filled with love, honesty, and self-worth; the life you are meant to experience.

"So what is an Alpha Chick?" you may wonder. An Alpha Chick is a spiritual being who has worked to deepen her connection with and faith in the divine presence within—your source of guidance, passion, and personal power—in order to meet life's challenges with purpose and strength. She is empowered to live a joyful life at her true and fullest potential. I thought of the term Alpha Chick several years ago as an appropriate way to describe my four closest friends. We all had experienced dark times in our lives and had pushed through them to live with purpose and passion. We are fulfilled and happy with ourselves, and our lives are rich and joyful.

I am telling my painful personal story in this book so you will know that I am similar to you—the symbolic girl next door. My story is a woman's story. I am just an ordinary woman, not a movie star and not fabulously wealthy. I am considered intelligent but certainly no genius, and my formal education was limited, as I left college in my first year. You and I may share many of the experiences that I reveal in this book; some of them we may have been too ashamed to reveal to anyone else. Yet I put my story on paper so you can see for yourself how I survived. And not only have I survived, I now have the most exquisite life and I am married to the man of my dreams. I am an ordinary woman living an extraordinary life.

When you read Part One of this book, you will see how I was able to overcome troubling and painful issues and humiliating experiences. Today I live a life very different from the one described. I am sober. I have fulfilling and meaningful relationships with my family and friends and a successful career. I run a multi-million-dollar real estate business I love. I make a concerted effort to take impeccable care of myself mentally and physically, and I am told I look great—much younger than my age.

As you read my story, you may ask yourself, "How did she do that?" Part Two describes specific practices you can follow to transform your life as I did. No matter what has happened to you or what you have done, you, too, can become an Alpha Chick.

My journey has taken me to an awakened and higher level of consciousness. On the way, I discovered a life-changing process that consists of five steps, which I call the *Alpha Chick Process*. When I deliberately repeated these steps over and over, my life turned around. This process literally saved me, and today I still utilize these same steps. The purpose of this book is to give you this process in detail so that you may use it in your own life. I will also tell you a little bit about other Alpha Chicks who inspired and supported me along the way. Hopefully, reading about them will give you ideas about what you can look forward to as you become an Alpha Chick yourself.

The steps outlined in the second part of the book show you how to recapture the self-love, faith, and hope you need to create a new vision for an exceptional life filled with well-being. Great teachers whose works I have read have influenced many of the ideas the steps contain, and I share some of their wisdom throughout. With repetition over time, the steps will lead you to a simple yet powerful spiritual practice of aligning yourself with the divine presence within you, whether you call that your soul, your source, your energy, your guiding light, or by some other name.

To help you make this lasting and permanent shift, I have created a free Alpha Chick Action Guide to be used for the steps outlined in the second part of the book. You can download your action guide at www.AlphaChick.com/actionguide. Please do so now, while you're thinking of it, so you can begin to take steps toward a more purposeful, passionate and fulfilling life.

I sincerely hope this book will bring you all the strength and courage you need to allow yourself to change your life, and the infinite wisdom to venture on the path to your own personal awakening.

Mal Duane
Framingham, Massachusetts, 2011

PART ONE

From Innocence

to Obsession

to Transformation

The Early Years:
From Carefree to Caretaking

I remember my sixtieth birthday well. Standing naked in front of a mirror, I did a self-assessment. Basically, I observed, everything was still God-given and where it was supposed to be (except for the well-placed shot of Botox in my forehead to prevent it from crumpling like an old brown bag). While I'd discovered hair growing in places I'd never thought it could and turning white in places I'd never thought it would, nevertheless I looked young for my age. I had lost fifteen pounds over the previous nine months under the watchful eye of Weight Watchers, dragging my tired tush to the treadmill every day. Though I'd worked with a personal trainer for five years, I had never given 100 percent until recently. I'd found the rewards to be significant.

I started thinking about how so much of women's self-esteem and confidence is based on body image. While I was working hard to keep myself looking as good as I could, I realized that I'd come to a place where my sense of self was no longer defined by how I looked. I was celebrating a life that was everything I had ever wanted and more—what a change from where I had been before! Now, when I experienced life's disappointments and sorrows, I knew how to manage those feelings; I didn't need to suppress them or numb them with alcohol. I had learned how to calm myself and relax, and I didn't need to drink myself to sleep. Over the years, I developed a process that led to these transformations, and I found myself thinking that if I wrote a book telling my life story and showing how I pulled myself from the depths of despair and dysfunction, other women could duplicate that process. The ideas started to flow and I was eager to begin.

As I looked in the mirror, my mind wandered back to my childhood and one of my fondest memories: the story my father had told me about where I had come from . . .

✳

My father was the center of my world. He invented wonderful games that grabbed my attention, and he lit up my life with his humor and imagination. As a little girl, I sat in his lap each evening listening intently to the remarkable tales he told me.

One chilly day when I was five, we were having hot chocolate after raking leaves, and he told me the story of my "birth." He explained to me that I had landed in our back yard in a minihelicopter on a very hot summer afternoon. I listened to every word with anticipation while dropping more marshmallows into my cup. I fired back what seemed like a thousand questions: *Who flew the helicopter? How long did it take to get here? Why didn't it land in Mr. Cardy's yard next door?* My dad answered every one. The helicopter flew on automatic pilot and was all set up to land in our yard and not our neighbor's because I was being delivered to my parents.

I believed every word and was so excited by this revelation that I couldn't wait to get to school to share the news with my kindergarten classmates. My best friend, Mary Elizabeth Crandon, was crushed when I told her the story because she had been told that she came from a seed that her parents planted. For me, my arrival by air was so much better than a mummy's tummy, the stork, or any of the other renditions of child delivery that I had been told about. I knew I was a very special child because I had come in a helicopter.

I now understand that my father told me that story because he had a playful and imaginative mind, and he understood my adventurous and inquisitive nature.

Throughout my adolescence, he stirred my imagination every chance he got. He was one of the best storytellers I have known. Simple tasks such as raking leaves and going to the hardware store became extraordinary when I was with my father.

Back then, when I was five years old, I thought my life was perfect. I was born in Boston and we lived in a beautiful brick-facade home in the affluent suburb of Chestnut Hill, Massachusetts. We had live-in help throughout my childhood; our maid lived in her own private quarters above the garage. We had a beautiful summer waterfront home in Cataumet on Cape Cod, with perfectly manicured rolling lawns and a circular driveway in front. My sister and brother and I each had our own sailboats and were given sailing lessons. By the time I was seven years old, I was sailing on Squeteque Harbor on Cape Cod. All three of us went to exclusive private schools.

My parents married later than most of their friends. My mother, Katherine, nicknamed Kay, was thirty, and Larry, my father, was a few years older. Dad had had a brief marriage that ended in divorce before he met my mother, but that was never spoken of. He was a tall, good-looking man, about five foot ten, and very fair—a real towhead. I look like him and have his temperament and sense of humor. He became stocky as he aged, and his hair became silvery.

My mother was petite and slender with lovely dark hair, what they call "Black Irish." She was always immaculately groomed and beautifully dressed in expertly coordinated outfits, usually in a pencil skirt and high heels. She shopped in the finest clothing stores in Boston. She never wore jeans or sneakers, and she told me she thought both were unbecoming to women. Mom wouldn't even go to the post office without her red lipstick. She was a fabulous gardener, and the beautifully landscaped grounds of both of our homes reflected her talent. My mother was also a superb entertainer and hostess—she was charming, calm, organized, and a terrific cook. People loved her gatherings and parties, although she was more reserved and proper than my dad. She aged well and always kept herself impeccably groomed and dressed.

I know people really liked my mother because all her friends went to her with their problems; she was their confidante and they trusted her. In fact, Big K, as she was known in the family, had an uncanny ability to make everyone feel like her best friend, although she herself trusted very few people. Many times I would watch her and wonder what she was really thinking. My mother was a very private person; those dark Irish eyes held a lot of secrets.

My mother wasn't just a socialite, though. She was a Catholic with very strong faith. As an adult, I was to see her faith carry me and other members of our family through some terribly difficult times and losses.

My grandfather Duane was fabulously wealthy. He had started out owning restaurants and convenience stores, and then made a fortune as the cofounder and owner of First National Grocery Stores, one of New England's first grocery store chains.

Grandmother Duane looked like a queen without a crown. I have a photograph of her taken by Bradford Bachrach, Boston's top photographer at the time, in which she is wearing two large diamond brooches and many diamond bracelets. She was a cold, elegant woman who had almost no interest in her five children. She traveled extensively around the world, and my father, like her other children, was shipped off to boarding school from the time he was very young. When at home, he was raised by maids, nannies, and chauffeurs.

Despite his lack of parental affection, or maybe because of it, my father was warm and loving to his own children, and I adored him. He had that wonderful ability to weave a story, and we wrote and performed hilarious skits together. Although he was intelligent, well educated, and spoke three languages, I don't believe my dad lived a fulfilled life when it came to his work. He graduated from Harvard College, where he majored in journalism with a minor in criminology, after which he worked as a criminal reporter for the *Boston Herald* newspaper.

The only times I ever heard Dad speak with passion were when he told me about his work as a journalist. One of his most exciting assignments in college was studying the high-profile, controversial Nicola Sacco and Bartolomeo Vanzetti murder trial in the 1920s. He confided to me that he thought the pair was innocent. He secretly showed me the boxes in which he kept all his notebooks from his reporting days and cautioned me, "Don't tell your mother about this!" I'm sure she thought this work was "low class."

Eventually, Grandfather Duane got my father a position in the more "respectable" field of marketing and advertising, which likely wasn't too hard to do since my father would bring the First National Grocery Stores account with him wherever he went. Probably because of his father's influence and connections, my dad's firm was one of the leading agencies managing the advertising for John F. Kennedy's senatorial campaign in the early 1950s.

My father inherited money and made more—for a while. He was a great provider for nearly twenty years of my parents' marriage. All the money he made was spent on his family. However, I don't believe he was happy about himself, where he was going, or what he was doing. He went to work because he had to, but I believe he never loved his profession. He had done "the right thing" by going into advertising as a way of providing for his family. He had done what his father wanted him to, but in doing so he had abandoned his own dreams and aspirations.

My father appeared very strong and dependable to me in my early childhood, but as I matured, my impressions changed. I think he was essentially not his own person, dwarfed by his father's shadow and ultimately weakened by traces of depression and drinking, as were his three brothers. Alcoholism was a thread woven throughout his family.

My grandfather repeatedly bailed his sons out of the trouble in which they found themselves, and as adults they remained dependent upon him. In 1953, at the age of seventy-six, he played eighteen holes of golf at the legendary Breakers resort in Palm Beach, Florida, turned to play another eighteen, and died from a massive heart attack on the golf course. His children were left with money, alcoholism, and failing marriages.

My mother's parents, Timothy and Katherine Hickey, emigrated from County Cork, Ireland, and settled in a modest colonial home in Brookline, Massachusetts. While not wealthy, it appears they were quite comfortable.

My maternal grandparents were two of the sweetest people I have ever met. When my mother would drop me off to visit them as a young child, I always knew that they were genuinely happy to have me there. I had so much fun on those visits! Grandfather Hickey played the piano, and whenever he played *When Irish Eyes Are Smiling*, I would sing and dance around the room, laughing and clapping my hands.

Their neighbor across the street, Mr. Getty, who was a firefighter in Chestnut Hill, had a wonderful vegetable garden. When I stayed at my grandparents' house after dark on summer evenings, I would sometimes sneak over to "steal" tomatoes and other goodies from Mr. Getty's garden to bring home to them. Of course, Mr. Getty knew I was the one who was taking them because my grandparents told him, but he let me get away with it and never once came out and stopped me. I would be so excited when I ran back to Grandmother and Grandfather Hickey's with my pilfered veggies! Those were sweet and easy days.

My grandparents were rather formal people in their dress. Grandfather Hickey always wore a freshly starched shirt accented by striped suspenders. My grandmother wore tailored dresses with nylon stockings and finished off her outfits with chunky black tie shoes. I remember those shoes and how strange they looked to me as a little girl. She also had something that was very fashionable in those days—a mink stole with the head of the poor animal as a clasp and its feet dangling from the other end. It was my favorite dress-up plaything in their house! Grandma would let me wrap it around my head and pretend to be an animal, growling at the two of them.

I don't have lots of memories of my maternal grandparents because Grandmother Hickey died when I was around six years old and Grandfather Hickey passed away about two years later. My mother usually controlled and restrained her emotions, and the occasion of her mother's death was the first time I saw her sob uncontrollably. The second and only other time was when we visited my father's grave shortly after he died.

I don't remember my mother playing with me like my father did—she seemed to dote more on my brother and sister. She rarely hugged me or comforted me physically. The only times I remember her holding me close were when we were swimming in the surf at the ocean. She would grab my waist and hold me tight against her, probably so I wouldn't be swept away by the waves. Mostly I turned to my dad for affection and nurturing. With Mom, I could scream, cry, or pull my hair out, but she wasn't moved in the least. Dad, on the other hand, would let me have my way—he had a hard time saying no.

I was born when my mother was thirty-seven. The youngest of three, I was the baby of the family. Although I had this precious title, I did not receive any special privileges along with it. I was lanky, with platinum blond hair and wide eyes. Frequently I cut my own bangs, which then looked like a broken picket fence. I was outgoing and sensitive to others, much like my dad. My brother, Larry, and my sister, Kathy, were dark-haired and mild-mannered compared to me. Born a year apart, they were almost like twins, and were always very close. Together they did their best to torment me. For example, for years they told me I was adopted, and until I got older, I was never sure.

In my earliest years, I was a happy child, precocious and gifted, with a wicked sense of humor. I loved animals and found my greatest comfort with them. I was always surrounded by furry creatures, inside our house and out. I brought home wayward animals and kept them in my bedroom. Once, four baby robins that had fallen from a nest in a nearby tree provided unique decorations for my room—from one end of it to the other, white droppings speckled the pink carpet. I'm still amazed that my mother allowed me to do this—it was the one time she didn't say no! Over time, she got used to my love of animals, but she never stopped checking my pockets as I came through the front door.

While my sister loved her Madame Alexander dolls, my passion was stuffed animals, along with the live ones. I was a tomboy and often wore my trusty six-shooters in a double holster. My best friends were the neighborhood boys. My only girlfriend, Mary Elizabeth, was a funny little kid who looked like a female version of the Jerry Mathers character "Beaver" on the *Leave It to Beaver* TV show. We shared a love of bugs, birds, and bikes, as well as a mutual disgust for frills, lace, and dresses.

I was very sociable as a child. By the time I was five or six years old, I made regular visits by myself to our older neighbors in Chestnut Hill and at our summer home on Cape Cod. Surprisingly, I was allowed to roam the neighborhoods alone at this very early age, except in the spring, when my mother warned me to beware of the Gypsies who came to Chestnut Hill to pick dandelions for dandelion wine—at least that's what she told me. I don't know if they were real Gypsies, but they did come every year in strange garb, and my mother told me they kidnapped children. However, other than warnings about the Gypsies, my mother wanted us to be independent; she discouraged her kids from being clingy, dependent children who couldn't think on their own.

From the very early age of four, often after dinner I would visit Mary Ferguson, the caretaker of the older gentleman who lived in the house next door. I would ring the doorbell and say, "Mary, I'm here for my Oweo cookie," and she always had one for me.

Frequently, when we were on the Cape, I would visit our neighbor, Father Johnson, an aged Catholic priest who raised and bred champion Boxer dogs. One day I accidently left my "pockey"—my small gold sequined handbag from which I was inseparable—at his house, and I was devastated. We never could find it, though we looked all summer. Father Johnson felt so badly about the disappearance of my "pockey" that he gave me a boxer puppy. I named the dog Jeffrey.

Making the rounds of our neighbors' houses by myself, I would make up the most insane stories to share with them and would gossip about everybody. In my wide-eyed, theatrical manner, gesturing with my hands, I would tell them about how other neighbors' houses were a mess or how I heard a family down the street yelling at each other and having fights. Everybody I visited knew my stories were fabrications, but they would attentively listen to me as I told them. What an imagination I had in those days!

Once, while talking through my missing teeth, I told them that I had "wrats in my pwayhouse." Everyone thought I had made it up, but this seemingly tall tale was true. I had put baby food for my stuffed animals in my outdoor playhouse and somehow the food had attracted rats!

To sum up my early childhood, while my mother didn't dote on me as much as I might have wished, my days were relatively carefree and full of adventures. However, this perfect world started to change when I was nine.

At six o'clock every day, my parents had their cocktails: two bourbon manhattans. All their friends did the same thing. Dad was always home for this. My recollection is that until I was ten years old, he remained in the city after work on only two or three occasions.

Then he began a pattern of increased drinking as his finances became more precarious. Since previously he had always come home at the same time, when he didn't show up on the nightly train in time for dinner, we knew he wouldn't be back until late at night.

On these first few occasions, when Dad finally did come home, he would be intoxicated. He would try to sneak into the house quietly, but it never worked. When he'd finally get the key into the lock and try to open the door, he wouldn't be able to get in—my mother would intentionally put the chain locks on the doors. He would walk around to all the doors, rattling them, which would cause Jeffrey to bark. Because my bedroom was on the side of the house near the back stairs, I could sneak down to unlock the back door and let him in. He would be unstable on his feet, his face flushed and his eyes glassy. He looked and acted very different—what was happening to my father?

Sadly, as I grew older and my sister and brother left for college, this occurred more and more frequently, and that look and behavior became all too familiar. His drunkenness scared me—it made me feel like my world was upside down and falling apart. There was a transformation taking place. He became a different person, sad and disconnected, needing help—not the dad I had known, the one who was supposed to take care of us. The man I loved so deeply was slipping away before my eyes. I felt I needed to take care of him. Sometimes I would heat up a can of his favorite Dinty Moore beef stew to make sure he had something to eat. Then I would help him get upstairs and into the maid's room, if she wasn't around, or into mine if she was. On the nights he stayed in my room, I slept with my mother.

So, at a young age, I became my father's caretaker, and along with that, I became frightened and sad. As a child, I thought something at home was driving him away. I don't know why, but I believed the problem was with *us* and not with *him*. If only we were good enough, I surmised, Dad wouldn't act this way. (This fear and sense of abandonment stayed with me for many years and resulted in devastating consequences in my adult relationships with men—I developed an inability to trust, and I felt responsible and compelled to repair these relationships.)

After these episodes, my mother would be furious, and for the next several days, she would make Dad's life hell. She would serve dinner to the children, but not to him. There would be no communication between them— she would act as though he were invisible and refuse to talk to him. She was the Queen of the Cold Shoulder, and he would be ridden with guilt. At these times, our home had a tense, heavy atmosphere for a young girl to live in. Unfortunately, as I got older, my father's alcohol intake increased. However, my love for him never diminished, and I still felt his love for me.

Most of my parents' friends also had pretty close relationships with alcohol, especially when we were on Cape Cod in the summer. Drinking was a way of life for that crowd. I remember one time when my parents were coming into the harbor after cruising around on a boat with a bunch of their friends—one of the men was so drunk, he walked right off the boat into the water! Another time, a couple of their friends who were on the way home from an evening of partying took a wrong turn and drove their convertible over the curb and right down onto the beach, where it got stuck in the sand. They had to walk home drunk and leave the car to be towed home. Some of us kids saw it in the sand the next day. We knew they had been looped and thought it was funny. This was a typical summer Saturday evening activity for our parents, who went to the yacht club parties, and we considered it to be normal!

In the 1950s and 1960s, prominent Irish Catholic families never discussed or even mentioned the word *alcoholism*. Today, we describe this as the "elephant in the room"—huge but unmentioned, a secret only to the secret-keepers. Now people openly discuss the disease of alcoholism and their personal experiences with it. Alcohol dependency is no longer a dirty word but a recognized medical condition, well defined, with highly sophisticated treatment options. For example, former First Lady Betty Ford, a self-admitted addict and alcoholic, opened a treatment center under her own name. However, during the time I was a young girl, the family disease model of alcoholism and the effects of one person's drinking on everyone in the family had yet to be identified. Nevertheless, it was the defining theme of my adolescence, as were secrecy, denial, fear, and sadness. As I got older, I was always uneasy, worrying about what might happen next.

I spent three years in public school and constantly got into spats with the kids in my classes. One time in third grade, I was playing kickball with a few other kids. One of them was a real nebbish named Morton. He picked up the ball, which you weren't allowed to do in kickball, and I yelled at him to put it down, but he didn't. So I went over to him, intending to kick the ball out of his hands because I wanted to play the game the *right* way. I wasn't feeling too tolerant of his cheating— even at that age, I wasn't afraid to stand up for what I believed in. Well, instead of contacting the ball when I kicked, my red-sneakered foot slipped and inadvertently went right into poor Morton's crotch, and he fell to the ground screaming and rolling around. All hell broke loose over this one! His parents called my parents, insisting I had done this to their precious Morton intentionally, which I hadn't. Who knows, I might have ruined Morton for life when it came to girls. Sorry, Morton.

By fourth grade, my parents thought a change of venue was in order. They hoped a girls' school would soften my tomboyish ways and sent me to the Brimmer and May School, a private day school in Chestnut Hill. As it turned out, Mary Elizabeth was sent to Brimmer and May at the same time, and I was really glad about that. Neither one of us was too keen on the idea, but at least we were together.

Mary Elizabeth lived nearby on Hilltop Road. Her parents were both doctors, which was kind of unusual for those times. Mary Elizabeth was pretty much raised by her rather inefficient nanny. Despite her parents' comfortable incomes, she always looked like a little ragamuffin, with stained clothes and torn hems hanging down above her scuffed shoes. We were the best of friends and had great times together.

One time when we were about ten years old, we were out in the neighborhood riding our bikes together. I took a bad fall off my bike and really banged myself up. My knees and legs were scraped and bloody, and I was distraught—I cried because it hurt so much. Mary Elizabeth ran to the house to get bandages and tried to fix me up and comfort me. I knew she cared for me and was really worried about me. She was a real friend.

I settled down in private school, made new friends, and loved most of my classes. At Brimmer and May, classes were much smaller than at the public school, with a ratio of one teacher to about ten students. The teachers stimulated our interest in what we were studying and gave us a lot of individual attention. The school had a great sports program that I loved. I especially liked to play field hockey and was quite good at it.

During the rest of my elementary- and middle-school years, I was pretty content and actually had a bit of self-confidence. I think it definitely helped that there were no boys around to make fun of me because my ears stuck out, like the boys in public school had. I was so tired of being told that I looked like a "taxi with the doors open." None of us were competing for the boys' attention, either. However, as I approached puberty and my teen years, the ways in which I was different from my contemporaries became more apparent. The roots of my inferiority complex and lack of self-esteem started to sprout, and a huge dose of fertilizer was lurking around the corner.

Mal-function

My high school years at Brimmer and May were pretty uneventful other than the fact that I grew eleven inches in two years, while in the tenth and eleventh grades, and had my first blackout . . . well, I guess they weren't quite "uneventful." My appearance changed very quickly, and as my looks changed, so did my life—for the worse. I reached five foot eleven, but I weighed only 105 pounds! I was flat-chested and incredibly skinny, with big ears and braces. I was suddenly taller than everyone I knew; even my older brother and sister were shorter. Some of my "friends" would tease and taunt me till I was in tears.

My summer friends from the Cape were my worst critics. They certainly let me know I wasn't a member of their precious clique. They didn't ostracize me, but they teased me and treated me differently from the way they treated each other. They let me hang around but acted like they didn't like me. They gave me horrible nicknames like "Mal-function," "Mal-nutrition," "the Celtic" (for the Boston Celtics basketball team), and "Big Foot." Because my ears stuck out, some of them even asked me if my mother had taken thalidomide, a drug given to pregnant women in the 1950s and 1960s to treat morning sickness, which was later found to cause severe birth defects. They were incredibly cruel, and I didn't handle it well. But there was nowhere else for me to go during those summers we spent on Cape Cod, so I was stuck with this mean-spirited crowd. Every day I took my small powerboat over to the yacht club to meet them because I lived on a different harbor. I sat on the beach with the three girls with whom I was friendly, and swam and had lunch at the club snack bar, yet I felt lonely the whole time. I never felt accepted by this group of girls; I was on the outside looking in.

There was a girl all the boys liked named Diana, who looked like a California surfer girl: short, well-developed, with long, straight, blond hair. I dreamed of being five foot two, with blue eyes and, of course, big breasts. I would have sold my soul to the devil to look like her. Any boy I liked was smitten with Diana. The fact that she had the IQ of a plant didn't detract them—they were not interested in her brain.

I felt hopeless. I wondered if there was a way my legs could be truncated to make me shorter. I actually went to the library at home in Chestnut Hill and researched a type of surgery in which a piece of bone is removed from each leg in cases of extreme growth. Of course, my mother would hear none of that! Because I was growing so fast, I actually had terrible pains in my legs, especially at night when I tried to sleep, and this went on for months. When I told my mother, she brushed it off as "growing pains" and offered no help whatsoever during the many sleepless nights. I don't think she believed me when I told her my legs hurt so much. Perhaps Mom had some problem with empathy—she couldn't see me as a developing and struggling child.

I really needed help. If only my parents had noticed how truly desperate I was for praise and encourage-ment—how much I needed someone to tell me I was OK, that I was loved just the way I was. But they weren't able to understand my physical or emotional *needs*. I don't think it ever occurred to them that a child who lived a comfortable life, with a summer home, live-in help, and private schools, could even have needs.

I wanted to look like the other teenagers and be accepted by them, but that just wasn't happening. Kids made fun of my looks, and boys joked about my flat chest. I was a classic case of the ugly duckling, with no idea that I would ever become beautiful.

Although my self-image was sinking, the foam rubber I padded in my bra helped me to float in the water like a channel marker in the harbor when I went swimming. I became a master of the art of fake boobs as a remedy for flat-chestedness. One of the most painful moments in my life was one night when my father exposed my secret at the dinner table. Thinking it was a great joke, he put my falsies on the dining room table, like a couple of dinner rolls, for all to see. As it happened, one of my brother's friends had joined us for dinner, and I was so embarrassed and humiliated that I was actually physically ill for weeks to follow; I couldn't eat without getting sick to my stomach.

This dinner-table "joke" was a huge betrayal from the father I adored. How could he who loved me do something so hurtful and evil? It just seemed so very important to me to have breasts in order for my daily life to be bearable. Why couldn't he understand that and be kind? These were questions I would ask myself many times in the coming years. In hindsight, I realize it was too many cocktails and a lack of sensitivity to his struggling daughter that caused this behavior. My mother may have understood the level of invasion I felt because she too had suffered from Dad's alcoholic misjudgments over the past several years. However, she didn't try to help me because she was either in denial or just not able to empathize.

At private school I began to make friends with three of my classmates—Joan, Wendy, and Augusta. They seemed to genuinely like me and always extended invitations to me for weekend activities. Overall, my classmates were more compassionate than the Cape Cod crowd, maybe because we were at an all-girls school, where brainy types cared less about looks. Several of them went on to Wellesley College and were in Hillary Clinton's class. They were intimidatingly intelligent, with 800 SAT scores. I kept them in stitches laughing at my humor and antics.

My pitch-perfect impressions of the faculty were legendary. We had a history teacher named Ms. Baron, who had a unique, high-pitched voice that warbled. I mastered her voice and movements, and my classmates laughed hysterically when I imitated her. I thought that if I were funny my classmates would stay my friends, so being funny became part of my persona. I didn't always target the faculty, however; often the humor was at my own expense.

Besides being funny, I was academically capable if and when I applied myself. I must admit that learning in Latin class about Caesar conquering Gaul to the left bank of the Rhine with his legions of soldiers didn't interest me at all. Because reading was difficult for me, I was placed in a remedial reading group and never developed a love of English literature. But I adored math and sciences, maybe because they were concrete and precise. I got good grades—for a while. I even thought about becoming a veterinarian. Unfortunately, though, my academic drive really fizzled as my father's career in advertising began to take a serious downturn and going to an out-of-state college seemed unlikely. The day I took my SATs in my senior year, I wondered, *Why bother?* I was terribly disappointed about not being able to go away to school and was consumed with thoughts of how awful my life would be living at home.

By now, my father was having trouble trying to keep up with our lifestyle: two homes, one kid in an expensive private school and two in college, lavish entertaining, and live-in staff. My mother never discussed the financial pressures he was under. She was masterful at managing money, so no one knew their true status because she kept on as if nothing had changed. Nobody talked about what was happening in our family. Then, when my father was in his mid-fifties, he lost his job at the advertising agency. Sadly, he was replaced by a younger man for half the salary he was being paid.

While my father lamented his loss of income, my mother quietly balanced household expenditures. However, I was fully aware of the challenges with which they were both dealing. Dad tried a couple of new ventures and investments that failed, and my parents began to argue more and more. The more financial stress my father felt, the more depressed he became and the more he would reach for the soothing mollification of a cocktail. I felt his suffering, but I couldn't help him anymore the way I had as a little girl. Instead, when he drank too much, I stayed out of his way. My mother stoically kept up appearances, and I had no one to talk to about our family life.

Both my sister and brother had gone away to college. At this time, Kathy was attending Marymount College in New York, and Larry had graduated from Georgia Tech and was attending graduate school at Emory College in Atlanta. They had escaped my dad's declining health, drinking, and diminished finances. I don't think they knew what was going on back home—my mother certainly never told them and neither did I. What was happening in our family was not a topic of conversation.

By the beginning of my senior year in high school, I knew for sure that I would have to attend a local college—an exclusive out-of-state school was financially impossible. I hope you don't think I was just another spoiled rich kid who wanted to go away to a posh school like her brother and sister had because of the status involved—that wasn't it at all. I *needed* to get away from what was going on at home—the drinking, the depression, and the arguments. There were plenty of good schools in Massachusetts, but I felt I wouldn't be comfortable or emotionally safe living at home. My father's increased drinking and personality change had made our house a hornet's nest for me. On the other hand, as much as I wanted to go away, I was also concerned about leaving my mother home alone to cope with all of this. I realized I couldn't. I was desperate, but I couldn't escape by going away to school.

In the fall of my senior year of high school, I discovered the comforting effects of Colt 45 beer. Sometimes I could just walk into my favorite liquor store and buy it; my height and upswept hair made me look old enough. When I drank three cans quickly, I would get drunk and not think about anything. I remember putting my head on my pillow while the room spun out of control—there was relief in that oblivion. I almost always got nauseous when I drank this way, and felt crummy afterward, but for me it was easier to live with the headache than the heartache. Sometimes I wouldn't remember much from the night before. At the time, I didn't realize that the terminology for this was a "blackout." Ironically, I didn't see any connection then between my drinking and my father's.

I graduated from prep school at age seventeen. I was a very late bloomer, and a few months later a miracle happened! In August, on my eighteenth birthday, I woke up with two bumps on my chest that felt like tumors. My prayers had been answered. Overnight, it seemed, I had developed breasts! I actually thought my life would improve just because of this, but unfortunately the fix wasn't that simple.

My new breasts and I started my freshman year at Northeastern University in Boston, enrolled in the medical technology program. The tuition was low, and they had a cooperative program in which students could work during alternate semesters. I tried to be interested in what I was doing, but within several weeks I was restless and uncomfortable. Living at home, I was so distraught about what was happening there that I couldn't concentrate on my classes or homework assignments.

To complicate matters, coming from a small private girls' school in the suburbs, I felt lost and over-whelmed at this enormous inner-city university that went on for blocks and blocks; finding my classes was a challenge in itself. Also, I had very little in common with my class-mates, many of whom came from blue-collar back-grounds. Once again, I didn't fit in. I wasn't a snob—I just didn't know how to talk to people who were so different from me. This experience was very unlike what I had hoped my college experience would be.

In truth, I never really made any serious attempt to socialize with my classmates—I struggled every day just to show up. I wasn't coping with my own life at all. I didn't understand the whirlwind I was in, as in those days there was no information about the dynamics of an alcoholic family, or even that there was such a thing as an alcoholic family, or how much my family dynamic affected the way I was functioning on a daily basis.

It wasn't long before I stopped trying to succeed at Northeastern. I had met one of my friend Pam's cousins, John Fuller, at her sister's debutante party at the Ritz Carlton Hotel, and we kept in touch after I entered college. John was a handsome trust-fund baby from Boston who looked like the actor Pierce Brosnan. He was the grandson of Alvan T. Fuller, the late governor of Massachusetts. Yet even with good looks and money, he wasn't happy. I was drawn to him, maybe because we had similar reasons for our unhappiness—both of John's parents had problems with alcohol. He became one of my escorts for my debutante party.

John and I began meeting late in the afternoons at the Saxony Lounge on Boylston Street in Boston. Two young kids who preferred a bar to college classes, we would have a few drinks before I went home from school. With similar backgrounds, we were great company for one another, and we both liked to drink. We would fantasize about how our lives could be better and give each other creative alternatives to what we were doing. Each day I got home later and later from school. I'm sure my mother could sense that something was going on with me, but she didn't, or couldn't, ask. I did little or no studying, and my grades reflected it.

Knowing my frustration with school, John told me how his sisters, who were also tall, had been doing some modeling in New York. I'm sure the fact that they were also drop-dead gorgeous didn't hurt. (In those days, when you were that good-looking and wealthy, your level of education could be overlooked. A year abroad study-ing Renaissance painters would be enough to *appear* educated, especially since looks were what it was all about.) John said modeling agencies would probably like me because of my height. I appreciated the encourage-ment, but wondered if he was looking at the same girl I saw in the mirror. I certainly didn't think I looked like modeling material.

Within a year, John was dead. He had been drinking one night with his brother Alvan. They were leaving one of their favorite bars near their home in Rye, New Hampshire, and Alvan wanted John's keys to the car. They got into a terrible fight, and John drove away alone at high speed. Tragically, he drove through a guardrail and his car landed in the ocean upside down. He was not killed instantly, but struggled violently to get out. Pinned underneath the steering wheel, he suffered an agonizing death by drowning—another chilling example of the toll of alcoholism.

Oh, if only someone had sat me down and told me that this was just a difficult time in my life, especially with an alcoholic father. If only someone had told me that I would have the spunk to get through it, that looks aren't as important as what's inside a person, that I could make friends who would truly appreciate me, that I had a reliable center in myself and could focus on my own worth, that I could make a genuine contribution to others and to the world. But no one did say these things to me. My parents didn't talk to me about what I should do with my life, let alone show concern about my feelings. Increasingly, they were having trouble staying emotionally afloat themselves. I was lost, filled with self-loathing and fear.

So I did the best I could to numb myself with alcohol from feeling such painful emotions. I didn't have any notion that things could or would get better. I thought my physical appearance was beyond help and that I was ugly. I didn't know that I was anything other than what I looked like. I didn't know what to do with myself or my life. My sister and brother seemed so normal—what had happened to me? I felt like a freak.

Perhaps this chapter sounds like a litany of self-pity, but I think it's important to tell you what went on in my family and how it affected me. I know now that much of the emotional desolation and the lack of preparedness for life I experienced during those years were the result of growing up in a family touched by the disease of alcoholism. However, I wasn't aware of it then. My parents couldn't teach me self-awareness or the life skills I needed because my father was suffering from alcohol and depression—and they didn't even know it. However, I do know that they truly loved us. We were fed, clothed, taken to church, taught to sail, and sent to school. On the surface we lived well, and maybe for years we looked like a healthy family. But we weren't the perfect, healthy family; all was not well. Our family was like a brightly shining apple with the insides rotting. Denial and lack of communication were the two key culprits in our household.

Just a few days after I turned sixty-one, I was hospitalized for an emergency appendectomy. While there, I had an inspirational roommate named Ruth. She was in her late seventies, and her surgery was significantly more serious than mine, yet she never complained. She was strong and wise. Two daughters, two sons, and a granddaughter came calling on this amazing woman, and I admit that I overheard their discussions through the privacy curtain. I was very touched by their loving conversations. There was a real *connection* between these family members. They knew about each other's lives with a knowledge that we just had never had in my family. Until I was in my forties, I had not established this kind of relationship with my mother.

What impressed me most were the conversations Ruth had with her granddaughter. The young woman, in her early twenties, shared her dreams and ambitions about school and a career, discussing her fears freely. She was so open in these conversations that you could tell she was used to getting good suggestions about her life. Ruth guided her gently, a slight nudge here and a small idea there. She suggested patience and hard work to accomplish goals. Her granddaughter also talked about her relationship with her boyfriend and its future potential. This young woman was well grounded in her outlook on life and seemed prepared for whatever might be ahead of her. Her self-confidence touched me deeply. Ruth had raised her daughters with care and loving direction, and now her daughters were raising their children to believe in themselves.

Ruth, you are an Alpha Chick! If I had had that kind of openness, support, and honest communication with my parents when I needed it, I might have traveled a very different path in the years after I came of age. On the other hand, if I had traveled a different path, I would not have written this book. Ernest Hemingway said, "The world breaks everyone and afterward many are strong in the broken places."[1]

*

At the age of nineteen, I started to develop a very familiar relationship with pain. Every time I got knocked down emotionally, I just got up again and waited with the expectation that another episode would strike.

The Merry-Go-Round

After my figure developed, I noticed that people started to treat me differently. Now I heard, "How cute you are, how tall—you should be a model!" The prep school boys I knew from school and the Cape, who formerly had tormented or ignored me, now invited me on dates. But their approval and interest that I had so desperately sought didn't mean anything to me now; I wasn't interested in them anymore.

This was a terribly strained time at home. My relationship with my parents had reached an awful point. My mother and I argued daily, and I know I am partially to blame for this. I'm sure she sensed that something wasn't right with me, and she may have had an idea about my drinking. But rather than approach me in a soft, motherly way, she would verbally assault me: "What are you doing? Whom are you with? I know you're up to something! Why are you out till one in the morning?" All the anger she had about my father's drinking spilled over onto me as we rode the family merry-go-round of alcoholism. I think she knew I was in trouble, but because of her own inability to communicate with me and her tendency to sweep things under the rug, so to speak, she wasn't able to help me. I resented her questioning and doubting me, and I would fire back at my mother with indignation.

I had arguments with my dad as well. His new business venture was not going well. The financial pressures continued to escalate in our lives. Our living expenses were high: three college tuitions, cars and boarding at school for my brother and sister, and two fancy homes. My father's salary dwindled in his new venture, and the money he had inherited from his father was now almost gone. Still, my mother could squeeze more out of a dollar than anyone I know. She had always had a comfortable lifestyle and that was not going to change if she could help it. She didn't want anyone to know that we were struggling, including my brother and sister, and I don't think they *wanted* to know. Home was a miserable place for me, and school was not much better.

While I was still in my freshman year at Northeastern, I realized I just couldn't go on with school. I wasn't studying and, consequently, I wasn't learning anything.

My mind just wasn't there—not that I really knew where my mind was! It wasn't too long before I quit school, and that was a huge relief to me, though my parents were angry about it. But I also regretted giving up; the lack of a college education only added to my sense of inadequacy and inferiority.

Since I was no longer in school, I asked myself, *What should I do with my life now?* I thought I might try modeling; it seemed like a good alternative to anything else out there. Other people besides poor John had suggested that I consider modeling. I talked it over with my dad, who knew Mildred Albert, the owner of the Hart Agency, the largest modeling agency in Boston. He thought it was worth a try. I called her and got an interview. I believe Dad had called her first to pave the way. When I walked into Mildred's office, it seemed like she stopped breathing when she looked at me. Undoubtedly, at five foot eleven and 105 pounds, I was the tallest, thinnest girl she had interviewed! She must have seen something in me that I didn't see in myself because she hired me on the spot. The "New Mal" was on her way, I hoped.

I enrolled in the Hart Modeling School and, after a few months, emerged as a very chic chick indeed. I had learned how to pull it all together—to optimize what I now knew were my very good looks. I had learned about hair, makeup, dress, carriage, and style. I had mastered false lashes and how to wear three falls (fake hairpieces) at once. The transformation was impressive. I had gone from being a preppy little nerd to a striking young woman who attracted attention whenever she walked into a room. The feedback that the world was now giving me was that I was stunning! For the first time, I loved what I saw in the mirror. There wasn't a trace of the "Old Mal" there—at least not on the *outside*. I still harbored deep-seated feelings of inadequacy on the inside.

My modeling career took off. Quickly and amazingly, I began working with the best couture designers in the world: Donald Brooks, Pauline Trigère, André Courrèges, Bill Blass, Oleg Cassini, and many more. I was definitely what you would call an overnight success. I had gone from being the Chestnut Hill, Massachusetts ugly duckling to a very in-demand model traveling internationally for photo shoots. It was like a fairy tale, and I got swept up in the whirlwind of my new popularity after all those years of rejection.

My picture was on billboards everywhere in Boston, and I was making TV commercials as well. One of my exclusive contracts was with Grover Cronin, a major Boston-area department store. I was in their ad on the inside or back cover of every *Boston Playbill*, the national theater magazine, for three years, and I was having a great time.

One of my favorite photo shoots was a magazine layout I did in Jamaica with two top New York models.

Shortly after that, the famous photographer Ted Poppelbaum photographed me roller-skating down Commonwealth Avenue in Boston for *Life* magazine, calling me the "United States Twiggy." The English model Twiggy was the world's first supermodel, a skinny kid with the face of an angel who became an icon in the 1960s, and my look was similar to hers. We shared a short, boyish, bob haircut, exaggerated false black eyelashes, and long skinny legs that dangled from the tiniest of micro-miniskirts.

When the *Boston Globe* heard about the *Life* spread, they also did a write-up about me as the U.S. Twiggy. My photographs were deemed spectacular. With all the current photographic techniques, I looked even better in pictures than I did in person, and in person I was now considered a knockout. I was the girl with a thousand different faces— each day I could be someone else. Being in front of the camera was like being an actress, and the best part was that I didn't have to be myself. I could pretend to be confident, alluring, mysterious, or any feeling that would grip me at the moment. My insecurities were well hidden by the dramatic hairstyles, makeup, and clothing I wore.

A number of designers, major-league athletes, and movie stars wanted to date me. I casually dated or simply hung out with ice hockey stars Derek Sanderson and Bobbie Orr, baseball great Ken Harrelson, and football notable Karl Henke, formerly of the New York Jets.

I met heartthrob actor George Hamilton when I modeled in a fashion show at the Ritz Carlton Hotel in Boston. He was staying there while starring in the play *The Star-Spangled Girl*. He invited me to a performance and dinner afterward, and sent a limousine for me. The play was a bomb, and dinner wasn't dinner—instead he took me to a wild party at someone's house in Boston. By the time we arrived, everyone was hammered. Before too long, I knew what he wanted from the evening, so I left by myself and went home in the limousine. Though brief, this date received some attention in the media, which asked about the "long-stemmed blond lovely running around with George Hamilton."

On another occasion, I was to appear at a poolside fashion show at the Somerset Hotel in Boston. I was running late, and as I pulled up to the hotel in my British-racing-green Jaguar XKE convertible, I saw a man standing outside in a dark jacket. Thinking he was the bell captain, I whistled for him to come over to help me with my bags. He appeared happy to help me as I got out of my fabulous car—a tall blond with a skirt about the size of a belt. A little later, during the fashion show, I noticed my "bell captain" sitting at one of the poolside tables, being introduced as James Darren. He was in town to promote his new TV series, *The Time Tunnel*. As I modeled by his table, I whispered, "I'm sorry!" Later on, he insisted I have dinner with him to make it up to him. He was very nice, probably married, and very flirtatious. I made another quick escape.

Although I may have been under the influence of alcohol on many of these occasions, I always recognized a man's lack of sincerity. And even though I was having the time of my life on one level, somehow their attentions didn't make me feel good for long. Through all this success, attention, and glamorous living, somewhere inside I was still suffering and felt profoundly insecure. Even with my wildly successful, adventurous life, I wasn't really happy, yet I didn't know why. I looked good on the outside, but on the inside I was sad and lost. This fast pace to superficial stardom fed my ego, but not my soul.

In the beginning of my modeling career in 1967, a few months before my twentieth birthday, I met my first serious boyfriend, Tony Athanas. I was having drinks with friends at Mother's, a watering hole in Kenmore Square in Boston owned by Red Sox team member Dennis Bennett and a couple of his friends. Tony was with his roommate and best friend, Tony Conigliaro, another high-profile Red Sox player, and they joined us for a while. With dark brown hair, bright eyes, and a beautiful smile, Tony Athanas was incredibly handsome and very suave. I was completely swept away—I got lost just looking at his gorgeous blue eyes. As an added bonus, he turned out to be taller than I am. But the evening ended without a mention of a date. I kept asking myself why didn't he ask me out, and later on I learned that he had been in a relationship at that time, which fortunately had ended by the next time we met.

Months went by before we ran into one another again at Sonny's, another Kenmore Square bar. Tony seemed really happy to see me, and I was thrilled to see him! I found our conversation incredibly exciting—I was mesmerized. The energy between us was highly charged; you might say we had a strong animal attraction to each other.

I invited Tony to accompany me to the Boston movie premiere of *A Guide for the Married Man*, starring Jack Weston. The event was a fund-raiser for cerebral palsy, and I was one of the guests of honor as the U.S. Twiggy. From the moment we arrived, cameras flashed to take my picture. Jack Weston himself came up to greet me, and numerous celebrities and men-about-town asked to have their pictures taken with me, among them the mayor of Boston, Kevin White, and the Massachusetts attorney general, Elliot Richardson. Tony was impressed and I think a little surprised. From my perspective, it could not have gone better. While I may not have done so consciously, I needed to impress him because I didn't feel confident, no matter how gorgeous I might have looked; I depended on my celebrity status and success to gain his interest.

Tony came from a very rich and influential family. His father was the iconic self-made multimillionaire Anthony Athanas, owner of Anthony's Pier 4 restaurant on the Boston waterfront. Pier 4 was one of the top five restaurants in the entire country and the place for politicians, celebrities, financial magnates, judges, athletes, and movie stars to be seen in Boston. Tony's father was a business celebrity with an empire that stretched to include several other restaurants on Cape Code and Boston's North Shore. Tony was his firstborn son.

We were an attractive couple just made for the society pages—tall, good-looking, and successful. While it was his looks that first attracted me, Tony and I turned out to have a lot in common. We both came from money and were at ease with each other in social gatherings. When we were alone, Tony was charming, effervescent, and engaging. We had long conversations, and I felt like he was truly a friend. We liked to do the same things with the same high-powered, well-known people. We both loved baseball and went together to every Red Sox game. We talked a lot about his restaurant business and my modeling career. We began to date steadily and became an "item." My parents liked him because he was educated, well-spoken, and respectful to them, and he treated me like a lady.

Tony was my first love, and I fell hard. I saw him just about every day from June until March of the following year. At one point when he was laid up with a back injury,

I went every day after work to his home in Swampscott on Boston's North Shore just to spend a little time with him. The trip was over an hour's drive each way. Somehow, when I was with Tony, all my fears about life vanished. I felt as if I had been rescued and that all was well. I didn't think about my dad's drinking, his money problems, or how awful I felt about myself—those problems disappeared just by my being with Tony. With him, everything seemed better. Even though I had my successful and well-publicized modeling career, I felt like I had no complete self when we weren't together.

For almost a year, it was as if my feet never touched the ground—I was so much in love with Tony—or at least I thought I was. Now I can see that there was a very superficial quality to our relationship, partly because of the times we lived in and partly because of the way I had been brought up. As I mentioned earlier, my mother was an extremely proud person who thought it was very important to keep up appearances. Her way of thinking included how to behave with men. She had told me many times growing up, "*Never* let a man know your business. And *never* tell him anything he can throw back in your face."

This advice stuck with me. Even if I had been able to put into words the bad feelings I had about myself or my sense of worthlessness and insecurity, I would never have talked to Tony about these things or about my father's drinking and financial troubles. I had been taught at an early age not to disclose "the real truth" about myself. And when I was with Tony, it was as if miraculously all these problems had been fixed and my life was perfect, the way it always should have been. I was twenty years old and didn't have a clue how a meaningful intimate relationship should be conducted.

Like most young Catholic woman in the late 1960s, I believed you fell in love and got married. My impression of romance was right out of the 1950s and 1960s television shows and movies. What I held in my mind about how my life should play out was a fairy tale. I wanted to be like the actress Grace Kelly—to marry a handsome prince and live happily ever after. I thought Tony really loved me and that this was it. Even though we never talked about it, in my heart I believed we would get married. Well, it didn't turn out that way.

Very suddenly, after ten romantic and passionate months of being totally lost in love with this man, Tony told me the relationship was over, and he didn't even give me an explanation! Here is how he did it: My sister, Kathy, got married on March 9, 1968. After the wedding, I went away to Florida with my Aunt Peggy for a week. During that week, when I talked with Tony on the phone, he seemed distant. When I got back, he suggested we have our reunion at a very public, popular nightclub in Boston. Obviously, he hadn't wanted to be alone in any private place. When we got there, he told me, "Things are changing with our relationship—we won't be seeing each other like before. I'm not going to be making a commitment to you, but we still can be friends." I think I stopped hearing anything clearly after the word *"changing."* How could this be happening?

Maybe I wasn't the right girl for him, or maybe it had nothing to do with me at all and involved some other issue of his. He never talked about his reasons for the breakup—he just did it. Maybe he had been taught not to disclose things either.

I have my suspicions about what might have happened. Tony had accompanied me to Kathy's rehearsal dinner and was supposed to be my date for the wedding. At the last minute, he told me he wouldn't be going. Shortly before this, I had learned that my father had gone by himself to Tony's father's restaurant, Anthony's Pier 4, and had had several drinks. Rather than drive home, he'd had to take a taxi from Boston to Chestnut Hill. I don't know that he had ever been there before—the restaurant wasn't a place where he would normally go.

Even before the breakup, I was horror-stricken when I heard about that night. I've always thought that while my dad was there drinking, he made some comments to Tony's father, perhaps to the effect that Tony and I would be next at the altar. It's possible he went there intending to talk to Tony's father about us, as if Kathy's impending nuptials made him think this was the thing to do. That would have put out in the open the hopes I had never expressed to Tony, and definitely would have put them out to the wrong person!

Regardless of what the real reason was for Tony's abrupt ending of our relationship, I was devastated. Based on my concept of love, I was an enormous failure because I felt I had somehow driven away the handsome prince (even if my dad or Tony or his father had actually been responsible). All I could think was that I wasn't good enough for him to want to remain with me. I put the responsibility for the breakup entirely on some failure of mine and assumed that it was all my fault. It was exactly the same way I'd felt as a young girl when my father would come home drunk. (What had *I* done wrong?) It never occurred to me that there was something to do with Tony that had brought this about, let alone that we simply were not meant for each other.

I was completely overcome by heartache and overwhelming feelings of rejection. The little confidence and self-esteem I had developed as a result of my modeling vanished. The bottom had really fallen out of my world, and I went crashing through. I was consumed with pain and didn't think I would ever recover. I can never find accurate words to describe how much anguish I experienced during this time or how devastated and panic-stricken I was.

I couldn't talk to my mother about my feelings of desperation. Her attitude was: "There are plenty of fish in the sea. Get over it." But I couldn't get over it. If only I had been prepared for the possibility that something like this could happen. Now I understand how a romantic relationship between two immature people often eventually ends, and how unrealistic my concept of love was. But back then I was shattered.

Some of my close women friends tried to comfort me, but nothing they said or did could soothe what I was feeling. As women, we are often not prepared to handle the end of a relationship or the accompanying feelings of failure. Birth control and the resulting "women's liberation" may have freed us sexually, but many of us still deeply feel we need to be rescued by a handsome prince. I can tell you that my need for alcohol progressed exponentially from this time because it helped numb the emotional pain I couldn't bear to feel.

Tony and I continued to see each other infrequently over the next year or so. I would show up at his apartment, or he at mine, and we'd spend the night together, but always with the understanding that the relationship was over. He, too, may have had a hard time letting go.

It took me a long time to get over Tony. Somebody else might have been able to get a better perspective on this puppy love and move on, but I was stuck. For twenty years after our relationship ended, I tried to recreate with other men the feelings I had had with Tony—I was looking for my lost love. Yet it was only after I became sober that I was able to resolve the feelings of loss I had carried for such a long time and make peace with this part of my past so that I could truly move on.

The balance of my twenties was a repetitive cycle of high living, romantic escapades, and failed relationships. Like a merry-go-round, I kept going around in the same circle with the same results. The only difference was that I got better at anesthetizing myself by drinking to manage the pain. Not every guy I dated was a jerk and not every relationship was a disaster—I have memories of some really special people who became dear friends—I just wasn't available emotionally or I would intentionally sabotage relationships. I would show up and perform, but inside I felt painfully separate and alone.

In my fourth year of modeling, I became director of the Cinderella Agency in Boston. My modeling career continued to bring me into contact with professional athletes and owners of Boston sports teams, and in the early 1970s, I coordinated the first line of cheerleaders on the field for the New England Patriots; they all worked for my agency. Being on that field every Sunday with the players and screaming fans made me feel better about myself again for a while. It was very exciting and gave a big boost to my self-esteem, if only temporarily.

At the end of the season, I was given complimentary tickets to the Super Bowl and invited to all the big parties. Drinking with Joe Namath and other sports glitterati was a lot of fun and made me feel really important. By this time, I was living high in a social whirl of people I'd never even dreamed of meeting—politicians on the national scene, sports figures, and jet-setters. My exposure had stepped up to another level. I received invitations to the most in-demand events around town. To the outside observer, I looked like someone to be envied. But the evil voices of insecurity screamed within me when I was alone. The only way for me to soften the noise was to have another drink.

One evening I bumped into Oleg Cassini at a fashion party at—believe it or not—Anthony's Pier 4. At that time, he was one of the most sought-after designers in the fashion industry and would have been around fifty-five years old to my twenty-two. I had a stylish bouffant hairdo and had been told I resembled "Baby" Jane Holzer, an actress and model, and the first of the Andy Warhol Superstars (people who appeared in Warhol's artworks and accompanied him in his social life). Oleg was tan, handsome, and very physically fit. He had been invited in the early 1960s to design the state wardrobe for First Lady Jackie Kennedy, and she wore the gown he had designed for her to her husband's inaugural balls. I was in awe of him!

I couldn't believe that the famous Oleg Cassini would be interested in me. But after we chatted for a while, it was obvious that he was *quite* interested. When he asked if I'd like to see him again, I responded with an enthusiastic "Yes!" He invited me to come to New York City to have dinner with him at his home. Oleg had been married and divorced two times by the time we met; I believe he was divorced from the actress Gene Tierney when I flew to New York to visit him. His house looked like a medieval castle, finished in dark wood and decorated with suits of armor. The walls were covered with photos of celebrities he had dressed: Jackie Kennedy, Grace Kelly, and numerous Hollywood stars. I could hardly believe I was there! He wined and dined me, and our affair began.

I saw Oleg several more times, and he was always charming and attentive. We went skiing one weekend with his impressive group of international friends, which included many of the world's richest playboys . Oleg and his set were elegant and fascinating. However, despite his attentions and jet-set friends, I soon decided he was too old for me and stopped seeing him. It had been a short, fun-filled fling with one of the greats in fashion design.

My romantic interests ranged from an Iranian billionaire and real estate mogul who had fled his country to keep his fortune, to a future politician and White House contender. Meeting this man was quite an escapade! One rainy spring afternoon in 1972, I was driving down

Commonwealth Avenue in Boston. There was this striking man in a belted trench coat on the side of the road, with the hood up on his BMW—his car had broken down and he needed help. I stopped and offered him a lift to the closest gas station. When I dropped him off, he asked if he could buy me a drink later in the day. At five o'clock, we met at the popular bar Daisy Buchanan's, my favorite hot spot. At the time I think he was just at the beginning of his political career. He was a little surprised that I did not know who he was. I must admit he was handsome. This was another incredible incidence of instant animal attraction that fizzled pretty quickly.

Because of the new birth control pill, by the early 1970s the sexual revolution was in full swing, and so was I! Sex was now safe, at least from pregnancy. Sex, booze, and rock 'n' roll were the themes of the seventies, and I made it a point to keep up with the current trends.

What a mix of characters there was in my life! I had only a few quick dates with some men and a few longer-term relationships with others, which always ended painfully. After being dumped by Tony, I didn't trust men or myself. Because of my wounded emotional state and my clouded thinking from drinking, I was emotionally guarded and distrustful. As much as I tried, I couldn't connect with people, especially men, in any real way. Now I understand that the quality of those relationships was a reflection of how I felt about myself. As sad as it sounds, I didn't know then that in order to love someone, you must first be able to love yourself. Regardless of my career and financial successes, inside I continued to feel worthless and empty. I lived my life on the outside and tried to define myself by external events and accomplishments. The "real Mal" was lost and numb in an alcoholic haze.

My modeling career blossomed for a few years. I did all the top-notch shows in Boston and some in New York. When the designers came to Boston to show their lines, they asked for me by name to model for them—they liked my look. They could dress me in anything, no matter how offbeat, and it showed well. These designers dressed me in their wildest outfits, and the women in the audience would shriek with delight when I came out on the runway. At a show at the exclusive ladies' apparel store Bonwit Teller, I was intentionally sent out with a dress on backward so the "neckline" plunged to my navel. The audience loved this, and the women applauded nonstop the entire time I was on the runway.

Although glamorous, modeling careers are short-lived—there is always someone more beautiful and younger coming up behind you. By the time I was twenty-five, my modeling career had begun to fizzle and it was time to move on. I wasn't getting the bookings anymore and my nightlife was starting to show on my face. After I left modeling, I had various jobs in merchandising and sales. After only two years, I became the number one United States sales representative for Economics Laboratories, manufacturer of Electra Sol dishwashing detergent and other cleaning products. Again more career successes, and my life went on with its flashy social life and parties.

I celebrated my twenty-fifth birthday at a private party at Daisy Buchanan's. They actually closed the club for this bash that the owners threw for me, and my mother came as well. The highlight of the evening was when they wheeled in a six-foot cake. The head of a male friend of mine, Toby, was poking out of the top. I knew in my heart what was coming next. I pleaded out loud, "Don't do this—my mother is here!" But they pulled a rope and the top of the cake collapsed. I held my breath. Completely naked, Toby jumped out of the cake and walked right over to my mother! With an enormous grin, he said he did not mean to offend her but that this had been planned for months. He slowly dance away in all his glory. I could not believe how composed my mother was. She simply said she was fully aware that streaking was the "in" thing at the time. I stood in a corner gasping, but my mother never flinched or even blinked.

I welcomed my thirties with another fabulous celebration, dancing the night away with my adorable boyfriend David at a surprise birthday party my sister gave me. David was charismatic and wild, and he loved to party. He was the masculine version of a social butterfly, with great looks and flash. Living for superficiality, he was perfect for me. The night before my birthday, we were skinny-dipping in his roof-top pool when I dove in with arms extended and smashed the middle fingers of both hands. When I arrived at my party, I was adorned with metal splints. As she turned and walked away, my sister said, "Mal, I am not even going to ask you what happened."

David was the first man who asked me to marry him, and I accepted his proposal. There was one big problem, however: he never ended a previous relationship in which he was embroiled! He had a girlfriend in New York whom he visited every weekend after he proposed to me, claiming the visits were to end their relationship by letting her down slowly. He'd been bullshitting women his whole life, and I was no exception. David dated other women behind my back and lied about all of it. Months went by, but our relationship never progressed. Like most of my relationships, this one was based upon sex and partying, and never got much beyond that. Because my self-esteem was so low, I let him get away with his deceitful shenanigans for way too long. I can laugh about it now when I think back to the freezing winter night I flattened his tires outside of a Boston bar because I knew he was there with someone else. I denied it vehemently, but I know he knew I did it—my behavior was certainly as a crazy as his! Miraculously, the day finally came when I'd had enough and I broke up with him. But I still hadn't learned that the men you meet in bars usually aren't great relationship material.

You may be wondering why I am including so much in this book about my failed relationships with men. When people think about how an alcoholic's life unfolds, they often think more in terms of the so-called low-bottom alcoholic—the person whose life falls apart in every area, including job and family loss, failed relationships, and ruined health. In particular, I think people picture a slobbering, pathetic, falling-down drunk when they think of a woman alcoholic. However, alcoholism manifests in many ways. While they are all potentially life-threatening, many of us somehow are able to hold ourselves together in one area of life while disintegrating in another. Until I was in my forties, I lived this kind of dual life.

Amazingly, my business life appeared very normal and was not impaired by my drinking or lack of self-esteem. I excelled at almost every job I had. I lived two very different lives, one in business and another one personally, with different personalities in each. I think I was able to have such confidence in the business arena because I could be anything that I wanted to be during the workday and nobody knew who I really was. My appearance carried me and helped with my success in business. My colleagues and clients knew only my professional persona, which didn't require me to share any part of my personal life—just show up, give a compelling presentation, and then leave. It also helped that I was smart and competent; I could figure out what clients wanted and convince them I was the best one to provide it.

I was a natural in sales. My sales presentations were likened to Cecil B. DeMille productions—attention-getting performances—though they always had substance behind them. Fortunately, I was able to understand and grasp the value of the product that I was selling and to present it in the most convincing way to the customer. Although I took some "sick days" when I was too hung over to show up at work, for many years I was able to control my drinking during the day and function quite well. The nights, of course, were a different story. I partied like a wild woman, and my friends did the same. My physical health held up for the most part, but emotionally I continued on a downward spiral, barely holding it together.

I am greatly blessed that I made good career choices and interacted exceptionally well with people at the professional level. I never felt threatened in a business situation the way I did socially. I made a very good living, owned my own home, and lived quite comfortably. However, I never made a total commitment to my work and the people it included until my life changed significantly, and that was to take a few more years.

Marriage and Martinis,
a Lethal Mix

In 1978, on my thirty-first birthday, I met Ken
Gayron, the man who would become my first
husband. I was celebrating with two
girlfriends at one of our favorite hangouts,
Charlie's Eating and Drinking Saloon on
Newbury Street in Boston. We were our own
version of Charlie's Angels, the sexy trio of
private eyes that was so popular at that time
on television. We were the center of attention
and we knew it. Ken, an athletic-looking
fellow, and a friend of his were standing at the
bar. They were obviously staring at us and
taking in all the commotion around us; they
were intrigued and wondering who we were.
Ken and others started sending champagne to
our table, and the bottles of Dom Perignon
were lining up. Ken did his very best to
impress us. I casually gave him my name and

number, not expecting to hear from him; I thought he was just another handsome player trying to hit on me.

To my surprise, flowers started arriving the next day, then daily phone calls. After weeks of chatting on the phone, we made plans to meet. He told me he was separated. I'll never know for sure, but I think he had one foot in and one foot out of his failing marriage. Again, I kicked off our relationship with a night to remember. I invited Ken to be my date at the opening night of the Barnum & Bailey Circus being held for charity, for which I had been asked to ride an elephant! A crowd was lined up for my autograph as we got out of my black stretch limousine—one hundred people I knew had paid $100 each to see me ride an elephant into the ring. Clad in a flashy royal-blue spangled body suit and with red plumes on my head, I was a magnificent vision—I truly looked like a circus performer. I think he was a little swept away.

Ken loved boats and bought one while we were dating, so I nicknamed him "The Captain." He eventually got divorced, and three years later we were married. I know my mother never liked him, but I wouldn't have listened if she had tried to tell me why. The night before our wedding, he went out drinking and doing who knows what else with a girlfriend of mine, but I was unable to recognize this blatant warning of bad times to come; I certainly couldn't see what it said about his character.

Our relationship was doomed from the beginning. Two people who loved alcohol more than each other were living under the same roof. We bought a house in Hopkinton, a lovely Boston suburb. Ken owned a Cadillac dealership in Milford, Massachusetts, the number-one-selling dealership for its New England territory. We lived the high life for a while before things fell apart.

Ken and I had been married for only two years when my dad died in October of 1983 at the age of seventy-three, and my mother came to stay with us for a while. By that time, my parents had sold their large home in Chestnut Hill and had moved to the Cape house. Dad's health had been declining for a few years before we were married, and his drinking had tapered off significantly. In the last years of his life, most of the financial pressures he had experienced were gone, and he had begun to enjoy his family and his life again. Our relationship was slowly rebuilding, and I was very close to him once more. I was starting to understand what he had gone through and how easy it had been to turn to alcohol for comfort. I loved my father dearly and was deeply saddened by his death. I know for my brother and sister to read about his struggle with depression and alcohol is difficult. They were not living at home when he was suffering most. So their impression of what transpired is different than mine. His illness caused confusion and deep fears for me as a young woman. However through all of his challenges, I knew he was a loving father desperately trying to do his best. Finally that illness released its hold on him for the last several years of his life and he died a peaceful man.

Ken and my dad liked each other a great deal and had spent a fair amount of time together. He had often sought Dad's approval; perhaps he saw him as the father he never had. Ken's parents had divorced when he was a child, and his mother had "given him" to her sister to bring up, keeping Ken's sister with her. As you might imagine, he had profound psychological problems centering on women. I think Ken kept himself and his drinking under control while my father was alive because he didn't want to risk his disapproval. But when Dad died, there was a distinct shift in his behavior. I think he was feeling abandoned again. He began to unravel emotionally. His drinking escalated and our relationship quickly became abusive and ugly. He began to stay out late and often came home very, very drunk.

At the beginning, when Ken was only verbally abusive, I gave it right back to him. But as his behavior became more aggressive and his drinking intensified, all the resentment and anger he had within, perhaps toward his mother, was hurled at me. He became mean and physically abusive. As time went on, I was fearful he would kill me. He collected guns, rifles, and pistols, and had a supply of them in our house.

Five or six weeks after my father died, two of Ken's employees from the car dealership brought him home terribly drunk and in a nasty mood. They told me he had drunk twenty-one martinis! Astonished, I confronted them: "Why did you bring him home to me like this? Do you realize what I have ahead of me now?"

Trying to be helpful, my mother, who had made soup that day, said, "Ken, I'm going to give you a nice cup of soup." As she walked toward him with the soup, he pushed her away, knocked the soup out of her hand, grabbed her arm hard, and shoved her down onto the parson's bench we had in the kitchen. He screamed at her, "Leave me alone! You're not going to tell me what to do!"

Terrified, I called the police—this was my mother! They came but probably because of his connections they wouldn't restrain or arrest him. Instead, they told his buddies to take him away. The next day, my mother's arm was covered with awful bruises. Ken had gone to stay at a friend's condo, and I told him not to come back. But I relented and let him come home for Christmas when he promised to be on his good behavior. Our first separation had ended, but the good behavior was short-lived.

Ken came in drunk and stumbling one evening. I pretended to be asleep, afraid of what any communication with him might bring about. In a rage, he sat down next to me on the bed and accused me of taking his cigarettes anyway. Opening my eyes, I said, "Why would I do that? You know I don't even smoke!" I didn't realize that he had taken out one of his pistols. He held it to my head and said, "You took them and threw them out, you bitch!" I started sobbing, and tried to reason with him. "What do you want me to do? I don't have them. Ken, you're out of control. Please stop!" Eventually he stumbled down the stairs, breaking things and banging around until he passed out.

We went for marriage counseling a few times. The psychiatrist we met with actually called me at home to warn me that Ken could commit acts of extreme violence while in a blackout and not even remember the next day what he had done. He told me I was in danger and to remove myself from the house so I wouldn't be there when Ken came home drunk. (My mother had returned to her home on the Cape by then.) Many nights, I took the two little dogs Ken and I had at the time, got in my car, and drove around for hours until I could see Ken's car in the driveway. I'd wait a while until I was pretty sure he had gone up to bed and passed out. Only then was it safe to go back inside. If I went in while he was still awake, he could smash the house to pieces and me with it! I would sneak in and go right to bed, as quietly as I could. But by this time, I wasn't really sleeping too well—I tried to keep one eye open until he was safely out of the house in the morning. It was nerve-wracking!

In January of 1984, I was knocked down by a forklift that was moving stock in a supermarket and injured a disc in my back. I was hospitalized for a few days and then returned home, unable to work for several months. My mother came back to our house in Hopkinton to help take care of me. By this time I realized I needed to get out of this marriage and away from Ken. I wanted to get my strength back after my hospitalization, get back to work, and get myself out of this awful marriage.

Despite my precautions, the explosive incidents were becoming more common. Ken was very strong, and he often grabbed one of my arms and twisted it hard. I was terrified of him. One night when he came home, he threatened to beat me and chased me when I ran up the stairs to the second floor. Thank God a friend of his had come home with him and intervened, telling him he was going too far and to stop. Again, I asked Ken to leave the house, and this time he moved out. I had finally realized that I was a victim of domestic abuse and violence.

While we were separated, Ken was vindictive and mean-spirited. He did more things that really scared me. Cars would drive by our house, which was on a quiet, lightly trafficked street, at all hours of the day and night. I'm sure he had some of his thug "employees" casing the place to check on what I was doing and to harass me. Sometimes he drove by the house himself. I called my mother to the window to look one morning when I discovered that he had sent some guys around the night before to take away my station wagon, replacing it with a rusted old clunker that had a dead battery. When I sat in the front seat to try to get it started, the ceiling panel over me crashed down on my head. I had to go to court to get my car back.

I was so frightened I had an alarm system installed at the house. When I happened to mention this to a friend of Ken's named Jerry, a kind of low-class wise guy, he replied threateningly, "You know, if someone wants to get in to get at you, there's nothing that can stop him." A week later, the brakes on my mother's car failed—they went all the way down to the floor. Fortunately I was driving and managed to get the car stopped without either one of us being hurt. This was scary stuff! I finally realized it was time for me to get a divorce. I went to court, initiated divorce proceedings, and got a restraining order.

Despite the abuse and violence, in the summer of 1984 I foolishly allowed myself to reconcile with Ken one more time. I did this because of advice I received from my parish priest after meeting with him to talk about my marriage. I told him everything that had happened, and his response was to tell me it was my duty as a Catholic wife to try to make my marriage work. He said I should be forgiving and give this man another chance. I now wonder how many women have been killed because they followed advice like that!

Maybe the last reconciliation with Ken was something I needed to do before I could fully accept how hideous the situation had become. Whatever the reason, it was a big mistake! Remember, I myself was drinking at this time and my self-care wasn't at its best. Ken had been back only a week or so when one night we were returning home after an evening out. He was very drunk and driving much too fast. I was really scared and begged him to let me drive. His reply was: "The more you talk, the faster I'm going to go!" He was driving a hundred miles an hour on a narrow wooded road. We missed hitting the trees on either side of the winding road by inches! I told him I felt sick and again begged him to slow down. He yelled, "Go ahead, throw up! I'll just go faster!" By the time we arrived home, I was *physically* unharmed but felt *emotionally* battered, and knew the marriage was totally over. A few days later, I told him we needed to put the house on the market and asked him to leave for the last time.

Our divorce made *The War of the Roses* look like child's play. I spent the next year putting every ounce of my energy and mental focus into trying to get that divorce. Ken fought me at every turn. You see, The Captain thought of me as an acquisition, like a fancy boat or car. I was his trophy wife and he wasn't going to give me up without a fight. I spent $30,000 on lawyers, and we weren't even close to an agreement! Eventually I didn't care about the money—I just wanted to start over. My emotional infrastructure was crumbling.

My mother lived with me periodically from the time of my accident until the divorce was finally granted. She accompanied me to court six times during the prolonged and horrible proceedings, and helped me so much during that awful time. When I would walk out of the courtroom sobbing and having the dry heaves, my mother on several occasions would say something like: "Mal, it's going to be all right. I know you will get through this and over this." She would say it with such conviction that I was able to believe her and take strength from her words. My mother had incredibly strong faith, and it really came through when the going was rough for me, or for her.

The last time we appeared in court, the judge told Ken and me not to show up in his courtroom again until we had an agreement. Desperate to get this mess over with, I thought of a scheme that I hoped would work. I invited him to the house for dinner, plied him with alcohol and great sex (for him, not me!), and then asked him to sign all the divorce papers that I myself had prepared. Thank God, it worked! On the date of what would have been our fourth anniversary, I was granted a divorce in the Middlesex District Court; my marriage was over at last. Several weeks later, Ken stopped by to present me with a $15,000 Rolex watch for my birthday! Maybe he felt guilty for everything that had happened, or maybe he was trying to buy my affection again. Whatever the reason for this extravagant gift (which I thanked him for and gladly kept), the relationship was over for me and there was no going back ever again.

At thirty-eight years old and divorced, my drinking kicked up several notches and I had frequent blackouts. Sometimes, for example, I would remember that I had been on the phone talking to a friend at night but would have no recollection of what we were talking about the next day. Other times, my memory would be fuzzy from being out the previous evening. In contrast, during the daytime, I was desperately trying to pull my life together. I had started my real estate career and loved every aspect of what I was doing. Despite the drinking, I was immediately successful and that felt great. I put my heart and soul into my work. I was in control of my career, but my private life looked like a shattered mirror.

The more successful I became, the more I lived the dual life. Behind closed doors at night I battled depression and self-loathing, and drank myself to sleep. Yet the next day I would show up at my office organized and able to close lots of deals. At this point, drinking was not feeling at all good, but I couldn't stop. I often had dreams about dying, but then in the morning I would get up and carry on. Alcohol was the only Band-Aid I had for the wounds I believed life had given me.

By this time, I had spent several years in therapy and paid thousands of dollars to my therapist in an attempt to feel better about myself and to figure out what was wrong with me. For all my time and money, the diagnosis of "Dr. Feel Good," as I called him, was that I was a hopeless romantic with low self-esteem. Wow, how insightful—just about anyone could have figured that out! He loved to listen to the stories about my social life and the crowd with whom I traveled. It became obvious to me that he was more interested in hearing about who I *knew* than who I *was*. Although he knew that I drank heavily, he prescribed an antianxiety drug for me. He was aware that I was taking it with alcohol and should never have done so. He never once told me he thought my drinking was a problem, because he didn't get it. Like too many MDs at that time, my doctor really had no understanding of alcoholism. He really didn't help me, nor could he, I suppose, and I had no idea how to help myself.

Today when I think about all of this, I realize how often I hear similar stories from other women who have gotten themselves into abusive and damaging relationships. Why do we accept the little crumbs that are thrown our way and tie ourselves to men who bring us nothing but grief and despair? And what is it in us that gets us into these situations?

I attributed my low self-esteem and sense of worthlessness to the "father knows best" thinking that had prevailed when I was growing up, an insidious and pervasive kind of sexism that devalued women at its core. But women's low self-esteem is still a huge problem in these times when women are supposedly "liberated." In some ways, not much has really changed. At least once a week, friends, colleagues, and even more casual acquaintances approach me to talk about their painful relationship issues. They may not be alcoholics, but they are living the same kind of abusive life I did when it comes to men. I hear many versions of the same story about a woman who gets involved with a man who isn't good for her and puts him on a pedestal; he becomes more important than herself. How do we get off this merry-go-round?

A Gift in Disguise

In 1987, per my usual style, I welcomed my fortieth birthday with lots of glam, glitz, and flowing champagne. As I dashed around town in my stretch limo with my heavy-drinking lady friends, I was pretending to enjoy myself. But this craziness was beginning to wear thin. How many more years could I party and drink like this? The next day I had my usual post-birthday hangover and a bag full of souvenirs, including a Smokey-the-Bear hat, the name given to the hats worn by Massachusetts state troopers! Interesting . . . but how did I get it? I had some recollections of a crazy night, including a blond, six-foot-five, handsome guy, but there were many blank spaces in my memory of the evening. I might have had an even better time than I remembered—or worse!

Because these lapses were occurring more frequently, it was starting to scare me. During my blackouts, small segments of time were just erased from my mind, a horrifying indicator that I had truly progressed into full-blown alcoholism. My behavior was humiliating, and scarred by meaningless relationships with men. I also had had a number of fender-bender accidents over the previous couple of decades. Looking back on my many blackouts, I realize that I am lucky to be alive, not to have died in a car accident or hurt someone else, and that no one had hurt me. I believe I was being protected, even though I didn't know it and was doing everything I could to self-destruct.

The so-called good times not withstanding, alcohol was depressing me more and more. Because of my blackouts, I would wake up anxious, guilt-ridden, and filled with dread when I couldn't remember all the details of the night before. It was an awful feeling not knowing what I might have said or done over the course of an entire evening. I felt like I was coming to the end of my life. I had an intuition that death was approaching. The drinking wasn't working anymore to numb my emotional pain, but I still wasn't ready to quit. I didn't know I was an alcoholic; I thought I drank because I was unhappy and it made me feel better for a while. Alcohol had a real hold on me, and evidently my drinking was pretty apparent to others by this time. One of my neighbors,

George, a recovering alcoholic, told me many times that he was keeping a chair warm for me at his Alcoholics Anonymous (AA) group. I was not pleased, and my replies were less than appreciative!

As hard as it might be to imagine, given my night life, during the day I was still able to do my work and do it extraordinarily well. I held it together until five or six o'clock in the evening, and then the switch would flip. Perhaps it was because I was able to function so capably during the day that my denial stayed strong for so long. I was employed, I was producing and making great money, I was a terrific saleswoman. *What's the problem?* I'd think. It was a crazy, precarious existence, and the balancing act became more difficult over time.

My forty-first birthday went by without too much fanfare—the normal (or abnormal) gathering of friends at the Papa Razzi restaurant in Boston, our latest favorite place to carouse. In the middle of the evening, I noticed an exceptionally tall, dark-haired, younger man. (It is interesting to note that in my drinking days I began relationships based on the way someone looked, and, of course, his liking to drink was a prerequisite.) We had a brief conversation, and I found out his name was Paul. As we did the perfunctory phone number exchange, he stared at me with a kind of smirk on his face. I didn't have to take off my clothes—he already had me undressed!

I had met many men in bars without expecting any future contact. Well, Paul, a very handsome young lawyer, must have liked older women, because the next day he called to ask me for a date. At forty-one, despite the drinking, I still looked like I was in my thirties—thin, fit, and dressed in very short skirts. I soon learned Paul was only twenty-seven! But he was unusual for a man his age—charming, educated, and very engaging company. He preferred nice restaurants and going to the theater to loud hangouts and the flashy set. To me, this made him seem very mature. You'd think with my past experiences, I would have realized I was stepping into another pathetic and hopeless situation, but I didn't. And of course, for a while we had a fabulous time together. I never thought much about how preposterous the whole thing was. Paul was so much younger than I was—did I really think we could have a future? When you drink, your reality is so upside down. Within a few months, I was about to experience a new level of rejection and pain that would ultimately bring me to the crushing, excruciating reality and absurdity of what I was doing with my life.

Paul and I had met in August and continued dating into the holiday season. I've since learned that the weeks before Christmas are very emotional times for an alcoholic; I think of them as hurricane season. My own personal hurricane blew in totally unexpectedly when my sweet and supposedly mature Paul stood me up for a date one Saturday night. I waited and waited and couldn't imagine what had happened.

He finally showed up at my place around midnight, explaining that he was sorry he hadn't made it earlier but that he had come by *to do the right thing* by telling me that he could not see me anymore because he had met someone else. Somehow he had managed to convince himself that standing me up and then showing up at midnight was honorable! In addition to the feelings of devastation, one of my first thoughts was: *How the hell did he fit someone else in?* It had seemed to me like we had been together all the time. Maybe I'd thought about him all the time, but Paul obviously had had other things on his mind. I cannot imagine how he thought handling this breakup the way he did was doing the right thing. My grasp of his character had obviously been way off— my vision had been completely blurred by alcohol.

The end of this relationship and the way Paul had chosen to let me know were the final blows to what little self-esteem and emotional control I still had. It wasn't that I loved Paul deeply, although perhaps in my alcoholic haze I had thought of us being together for a long time. It was more the abruptness of his rejection that did me in. I had been in too many of these awful situations where I ended up feeling horrible and lost and alone. I was hammered when he arrived, and after he left I continued to drink nonstop for about forty-eight hours. I was on a real bender. But my liquid anesthesia wasn't working.

This was the lowest point I had come to in my drinking. My face was bloated and my eyes almost swollen shut. At the end of the two-day binge, I looked older than twenty years later while writing this book. I was shaking, sick, and terrified. My nerves were raw, and the emotional pain was way more than I could handle. The dreams I'd been having lately of death were almost becoming a reality. I had finally hit bottom, and somehow I knew that if I didn't stop drinking I would die.

My bottom was an emotional breakdown. Fortunately, I didn't end up lying in a ditch like some alcoholics do— as I could have. What I had was a complete emotional unraveling. I was so broken that a part of my identity died, which miraculously allowed me a critical insight into my life. I believe I was suddenly able to hear a new voice speaking to me in my mind, a voice that saved my life by allowing me to face the truth about myself.

What had changed for me that I had such a profound reaction to being dumped by Paul? I'd had many failed relationships, but this was the one that broke my spirit. I came to the edge of my sanity and I could not go on. In AA, they say sobriety comes by the grace of God. I believe that the grace of God was at work in my life at this terrible time because somehow, with almost blinding clarity, I saw the game I had been playing with men all these years. I saw the truth of all of it—the intensity of emotions I had wasted in destructive relationships with losers, users, and abusers. I saw that I was a bigger emotional mess after each relationship. I saw the pattern of lame, empty relationships I had gotten into trying to replace Tony and, maybe even in some way, my father.

In an incredible moment of awareness, I understood that these temporary fixes with men to try to feel good about myself had never worked and never would. All they did was leave me full of self-hatred, shame, and desperation. With the speed and power of a lightning bolt, I realized I didn't want to do this anymore and that to stop it I had to end this whole dreadful game with men and drinking. I saw death ahead of me if I didn't give up the game, and I now knew, when I wasn't sure before, that I wanted to live.

Surely God's grace flowed into my life again at the moment I first asked for help. I called my mother and told her what had happened with Paul. I explained that I was feeling overwhelmed and very frightened. I told her I was in real trouble. I am certain she heard the panic and desperation in my voice because she got in her car and immediately drove up from the Cape to stay with me. I told her I was very, very scared and that I was afraid if I drank I would die. She comforted me, not in a pitying, sentimental way, but by telling me, as she had when I was getting divorced from Ken, that I was strong and could get through this awful time—that I could get over it and have a good life and that she would help me. Despite her reserved Irish manner, which sometimes seemed cold, and the critical tone she may have taken with me as a girl, I now realized at this moment that my mother loved me and would be there if I needed her. I really needed her that night and in the days that followed, and she came through for me with all her maternal strength and determination. I am not sure what would have happened to me if she had not been there.

My mother stayed with me at my house and we managed to get through Christmas together. Though I was barely keeping any food down, she made meals for me and made sure I ate. I cried, I agonized, but I didn't drink. My mother suggested we spend New Year's Day together at the family house on the Cape and have baked stuffed lobsters—she would help me keep going for sure!

It was December 30, 1988, and I had two real estate closings to attend. My mother headed back to the Cape and I planned to join her the next day. After the closings, I went to lunch at Victorio's in Milford, where the two bartenders knew me as a regular. It was their idea to make me "mudslides" to celebrate the New Year, but it was my idea to drink them. Mudslides taste like ice cream but have the effects of jet fuel. Even after all I had been through, the most natural thing for me to do as an alcoholic was to drink, which I did nonstop from one-thirty to five that afternoon. I was blitzed.

When I got home, something in me woke up and I immediately said to myself, *This is it. I'm done.* I was tired of being sick and tired. At seven o'clock that evening, I rang my neighbor George's bell and asked if the AA chair was still available. The grace of God had enabled me to ask for help again.

George was a member of both AA and NA (Narcotics Anonymous). That night, he took me to my first twelve-step meeting, which he was chairing in the basement of a church. Though it was an NA meeting, I *knew* I was in the right place. I heard that I was powerless over my drug, alcohol, and *knew* that this was true. While still drunk from the mudslides, I tried to sell a condo to an addict sitting nearby whose glassy eyes were rolling in his head! Going to that meeting was the most momentous event of my life. Nevertheless, after returning home and going to bed, I woke up at three o'clock in the morning and had several sips of a Miller Lite beer because I was so thirsty. But that was the end of it—the early morning hours of December 31, 1988 would end up being the last time I would touch alcohol. I would never be under its influence again.

Later that morning I went to my second twelve-step gathering, this time an Alcoholics Anonymous meeting, which was being held at the Erich Lindemann Center in

Boston. I got as far as introducing myself—"My name is Mal and I'm an alcoholic"—and then I began to sob. I listened to everything the other people said and then went to lunch with a group from the meeting. They consoled me and shared with me that each of them had felt the same pain I was now feeling when they entered the program.

That day I also called my mother and talked with her about how desperately I needed help with my drinking. I explained that I wanted to begin the recovery process by following AA's recommendation of attending AA meetings every day for the next thirty days and didn't think I should go to the Cape. God bless her—she said she thought I wasn't that bad and asked if I really needed to do all that, but underneath I'm sure she understood.

The third meeting I attended was in Portsmouth, New Hampshire, on New Year's Day, and five hundred people showed up! I heard a marvelous as well as legendary speaker, John "The Indian," who had formerly lived on the streets of New York, covered with sores. Because he had been a drunk, I could identify with him, and I understood his pain when he told his story. I began to feel at home in the basements of those churches where the meetings were held; I'd found true acceptance for the first time in my life.

And so my recovery from alcoholism and my life in sobriety began. I went to meetings, I cried, and I came to grips with the fact that I was an alcoholic. I did just what the program told me to do. I got down on my knees every day and asked God to heal me and help me not to drink just for that day. I let go of *my* will and allowed a higher power to direct me. It was such a relief to be with people who had felt as miserable and hopeless as I did, and for the same reason, and who had found a way out. Amazingly, after drinking daily for twenty years and very heavily in recent years, I was able to put down alcohol without the DTs (delirium tremens—delirium caused by withdrawal) or a rehab program. With the help of people who had gone before me in AA, I began to learn how to live without the crutch of alcohol.

My opinion and understanding of God changed dramatically from my Catholic upbringing. I no longer feared God and didn't feel I was always being punished. I learned over time that I was created in his likeness and that through him I could live a life of joy and filled with inspiration. God became my guidance; daily I listened for my messages (lessons). I became extremely spiritual, though not necessarily religious. That is why I often refer to God as my "higher power," and I am telling you this because many of you may also connect to a "higher power" rather than to a particular religious deity.

The day sweet, adorable Paul said he couldn't see me anymore turned out to be a great gift. You may not believe it, but five years later, without having heard from him in all that time, Paul called me to ask if I would put a good word in for him with a new lady he was courting who also worked in real estate! I took that opportunity to thank him for what had happened in our relationship and explain that it had put me on the path to sobriety. He listened, but I don't think he had any idea what I was talking about. Fortunately, his new real estate love never asked me for a reference.

My PMS—
Positive Mental Shift

On December 31, 1988, the wrecking ball had made its final pass on the demolition of my life. I was no longer hammering in sharp nails of self-destruction. I now lived my life in twenty-four-hour increments and wondered if I could just make it to the next twenty-four hours. I was emotionally naked, a mass of raw nerves and feelings. Yet in spite of being at this vulnerable low point, I had hope and faith for the first time in my life.

I felt enormously blessed that I'd found the program of Alcoholics Anonymous and was getting it. In sobriety, I began to tap into a strength I never knew I had. There was a new voice in my head, leading me ever so gently. I would sit quietly and meditate for hours just to connect to this source of energy moving through my body and guiding me.

I started to see things in a different light, with new clarity about what I needed to do for myself. My former sense of despair shifted to an enormous sense of commitment to my own life and to anything I could do to support my sobriety. I had never experienced this kind of determination until I became sober. I had been running the race of life with one leg and one hand bound. Unbound from alcohol and men, I was no longer crippled by drinking or self-destructive relationships. I began to feel liberated. I received an amazing gift and have remained sober since that first day.

During my first few years of sobriety, I focused on attending meetings, following the AA program, and living life in the middle of the road emotionally. No more highs and lows for me; I had been there and didn't want to go back. I wanted to live a balanced life and build on what I was now learning. I didn't go out drinking. Instead, I made new friends who didn't drink, and found different places to go. My dear friend Cindy, who had been my best drinking buddy, had become sober before me and already had a year in the program. Before my marriage to Ken, we had shared back-to-back condos in Brookline, Massachusetts. Now she became my sponsor in my recovery. I talked with her daily about the challenges of sobriety and how to meet them without drinking.

Amazingly, the man who was to become my husband in 2003 happened to be one of the speakers at the AA meeting that I attended at the Erich Lindeman Center in Boston on New Year's Eve Day in 1988! However, I did not meet him until many years later. Who could have guessed at that time what was in my future?

There were simple steps to follow: attend meetings daily, drink no alcohol, and have no serious relationships for the first year or so in recovery. I must admit that at first it felt like I was trading one addiction for another. My new addiction was to get sober and get well, and I jumped with both feet into the pool of self-help. I attended AA meetings faithfully and established connections to people who had long-term sobriety. I followed the rules explicitly. I did what the program recommended and began to get well mentally and spiritually. I experienced a sense of inner calm and freedom that I had not felt since childhood, and those feelings have stayed with me ever since. More than two decades have passed without my needing to have a drink attached to me like a mitten on a clip. I was fortunate to have my work during this time, and I gave myself wholeheartedly to working with my real estate clients, a commitment I have maintained into the present.

I spent my evenings going to meetings or browsing bookstores for literature on relationships, addiction, and self-esteem. I read many books and listened to hundreds of taped programs about improving and reconstructing my life. In the process, I established a large collection on similar subjects. (Today I call it my Library of Love and give items away to those in need.) Slowly, there was a progressive shift in my feelings about others and myself. The rose-colored glasses were off and I was looking at things with an insight that was unfamiliar to me. I started to identify the most important areas of my life that had been affected by my twenty-four years of drinking. I accepted all my mistakes and was prepared to make amends to all the people I had wounded by my bad judgment.

Over time I discovered the works of an array of inspirational spiritual teachers, all of which gripped me. From Napoleon Hill I learned that thoughts were things. Norman Vincent Peale spoke about the power of our thinking. Eckhart Tolle taught me about the destructive thinking of the ego. Louise Hay showed me the effectiveness of affirmations in recovery. I learned from Ernest Holmes that we are all one with God, and Abraham Hicks introduced me to the Law of Attraction. I became an avid believer in this universal metaphysical principle, which was later brought to public attention by the 2006 international hit film *The Secret*.

The Law of Attraction defines how things happen in your life. It states that your mental images and the feelings connected to them manifest in your life as your reality. Every person, circumstance, and event that is in your life you have drawn or "attracted" there by the beliefs you hold in your mind. And, by extension, if you change your thinking patterns and processes, you can indeed change your life, as Ernest Holmes so adamantly stated.

Be assured, I knew nothing of this philosophy during my drinking days and would have found it preposterous if anyone had suggested it to me. Sobriety has given me the opportunity to learn new ideas and apply them to my daily life in very powerful ways.

Looking back, I see how the Law of Attraction has shown up in my life over time. As a young child, I experienced an awful feeling in the pit of my stomach when I thought I was going to be abandoned or when I wasn't treated the way a child should be (as when my father would come home late and drunk). I felt I was unwanted. As I grew up, I experienced that same nauseating pain a great deal of the time. In my teens, I consistently felt that I did not fit in, that I was unwanted and an outcast among my peers—the thoughts that ran through my mind as a child continued to appear *concretely* again and again.

This process continued through my relationships with men. Maybe because I had been let down by the first important man in my life, my dad, I always felt men were not trustworthy. I was afraid they would leave me for another woman because I wasn't good enough to hold them, and this image became my reality. For the first forty or so years of my life, as previous chapters describe,

I attracted many negative people and situations, especially relationships with men. And so it went, year after year, leaving a trail of disappointing breakups and heartbreak.

On the other hand, because I felt I could be someone else in my work, the negative thoughts I had about myself in my private life didn't interfere in that arena. The Law of Attraction allowed me to achieve success in business because I *knew* I could—I drew it to me like a magnet. It really is that simple, though this is not to say that it is *easy*. It requires constant vigilance and monitoring of thoughts and beliefs to keep them empowering rather than disempowering.

When I finally asked for healing and help from God, I opened a channel in the universe for better things to come my way. When I became sober and developed a genuine sense of self-worth, my perceptions began to change. I learned that I was a loving, desirable woman and that people would be blessed to have me as a friend. My newfound self-esteem created a new vision of my reality. I gradually began to view myself as a whole person, and consequently the thoughts I put out into the universe became healthier. As a result, the quality of the relationships I experienced improved exponentially. As I approached my mid-forties, I attracted better and better circumstances and people into my life. I started to make real friendships and dated good and decent men who knew me for who I was and valued me. Today I can see that the quality of my relationships directly reflected my beliefs about myself.

In 1993, I met Mark, my friend Sue's brother-in-law. This was my first appropriate relationship as a sober woman, and I didn't meet him in a bar! Sue thought we would like each other and arranged for us to meet. Mark was a kind, gentle soul with a great love of animals. He was incredibly warm and engaging. He had been quite a glamour boy in his younger days, and people referred to him as the movie star of Framingham, where I lived. The son of a legendary restaurateur, like Tony, he, too, had been raised in a family that suffered from alcoholism. I was comfortable being with him and not drinking; that was foremost for me. He would have a drink before dinner and, on occasion, maybe a second one, but he never abused alcohol because of his own upbringing and his father's drinking.

At our first meeting, I found Mark very attractive, but what really intrigued me was the aura around him of genuine loving-kindness. Although we were definitely attracted to each other, we were *not* drinking buddies and our relationship wasn't based on partying. We had many things in common and shared an interest in animals, especially horses. Mark owned several show horses and a couple of goats, and I soon discovered that he was one of the top breeders and showers of Morgan horses. He introduced me to how beautiful the horses were and what a joy they can bring to people. The Morgan horse, an affordable American breed, has a proud carriage and a graceful and muscled body. They are known for being calm, gentle animals with great flexibility in the ring.

My mother happened to tell me one day that she thought I worked too much and needed a hobby. I went on a trip with Mark to Maine to see the famous trainer Rick Lane, who was considered the best for working with Morgan horses. As I stood by the horse ring, I watched a spirited seven-month-old colt run to me and then quickly run away. There were a couple of other colts in the ring, but only this one was interacting with me, playing a game. He kept running over to where I was standing, then running away, glancing back each time to make sure I was watching him. He would look right at me, and I was mesmerized by his eyes. This lasted for about thirty minutes before I decided I had to have him. So I bought him!

My horse, Cabot French Cuffs, nicknamed Scooter, wasn't exactly the kind of hobby my mother had in mind, but he was perfect for me. This may have been an impulsive decision, but it wasn't a frivolous one—I had responded to my heart. I was now able to take care of something outside of myself and had found a really special animal. Scooter was a show horse, chestnut colored with white socks and a black mane and tail. He was gorgeous, and I could see he had the makings of a champion. My mother told me she was afraid I would be killed because, as she put it, "I did not know what end to feed." But I would learn, and learn well—I was growing as a person in so many ways.

I first boarded Scooter in Maine, but eventually he lived in Mark's barn and I could see him all the time. My mother came there once to meet him. Unfortunately, because he hadn't been exercised yet that day, Scooter was a little too frisky and wild. When my mother approached him, he reared up on his hind legs. She was terrified! Unbelievably, she hit him on the side of the head with her handbag, and the poor horse was dazed. I never remember my mother moving so fast as when she ran out of that barn, jumping up and down in the dirt! She had pulled her pencil skirt up to her nylon-stocking-covered thighs so she could run faster. Even today I get tears in my eyes from laughing when I think about this incident.

About a year later, another special creature entered my life. I have always loved dogs, and for some reason, I had begun to envision myself with a playful little terrier. I had actually cut a picture of a dog out of a Victoria's Secret catalog and carried it with me for several years, eventually learning that it was a Jack Russell terrier.

Then in 1994, I met Harley, who turned this dream into a reality. While Mark and I were attending a horse show in Oklahoma City, I saw a couple with two beautiful Jack Russell puppies. They told me they had bought them from a breeder in Yukon, Oklahoma. After the show, Mark and I drove out to visit the breeder to look at her remaining puppies. I picked out a tricolor puppy from the litter, but as I was walking out the door, something made me turn back to look at a little brown and white one. I sat down and Harley (the name Mark and I later gave him) climbed up into my lap. I knew at that moment that he was my dog.

Harley and I were inseparable for the next fifteen years, eating breakfast together most every day. This little furry fellow with his endless energy brought me so much comfort and joy. We loved each other unconditionally and were best buddies. No matter what was happening in my life, when I snuggled with Harley on his big red pillow, I always felt better.

Unfortunately, in the winter of 2009-2010, Harley started showing signs that he was tired and starting to fail physically. I promised myself I would never let him suffer and would make the best decision for the dog, even if it broke my heart. Because I loved him so much, I needed to let him go. He was euthanized on March 10, five months short of his sixteenth birthday, while curled up comfortably in my arms. Now in the morning, I pick up his big red pillow and just hug it; it is so difficult not seeing his sweet face. I have to keep reminding myself that I was blessed with his company for many wonderful years and that one day should not take away all the memories of love and joy we shared for so long.

Like Harley and Scooter, my mother was very important in my healing experience. She played a significant role in my early sobriety, and she walked with me through all the steps of the process for the next several years. She would come to my aid as soon as I called, and I learned to accept her help. From the beginning of this new chapter in my life, Mom was a master at instilling balance and structure in my daily schedule. We got up early, had three meals a day, and went to bed at a reasonable time. We both liked shopping and had many a hilarious shopping spree together. Unequivocally, my mother was the best shopper I have ever known (I might be the second best). Mom always negotiated, and I remember my niece, Holly, describing her determination for the lowest-price deals available as "Nana's School of Economics." Holly received a firsthand education in "economics" every summer in Cataumet when she visited with my mother.

I did not fully appreciate my mother until I became sober. Though I loved her dearly, we could really argue and end up saying terrible things to one another. Who knew we were two Alpha Chicks battling it out? Now when I look back, I know she was my very first exposure to a real Alpha Chick. Mom was emotionally strong, and she handled everything that happened to her with grace and dignity. Even when she was very upset with my father because of his drinking, she never really lost it— it was more that she was disgusted by what she thought was a sign of weakness. I think my dad's bouts with drinking and depression forced her to emerge as the strong one in the family. She was always a pillar of strength for us and for her friends. She never showed a sign of being rattled or overwhelmed. Of course I often ran the other way when I was younger because she intimidated the hell out of me with her honesty and wisdom. But later in my life when I needed her, she was there. She tried unfailingly to instill persistence and courage in me.

During the first several years of my sobriety, my mother helped me pick up the pieces of emotional despair I was experiencing and put myself back together. For example, just before I met Mark, I was in a relationship with another man younger than myself, whom I liked very much. When I ended the relationship because I knew it wasn't good for either of us, I was sad. I told my mother how much I missed him, and her response was: "Mal, let me take you to Falmouth Harbor for a lovely lobster on the patio." (Clearly, my mother believed in the healing effects of eating lobster!) While we were having dinner, I told her again how badly I was feeling, and she said, "Mal, mark my words. Someone will come into your life. Someone will be there for you who will really understand you and appreciate you for your extraordinary inner beauty. Most of the losers you pick only see the outside." In sobriety, I was able to hear the love and encouragement in my mother's voice. She didn't sound tough and cold anymore. It was only three months later that I met Mark!

This loving bond with my mother was one of the greatest gifts I received as a result of my struggle with alcoholism; it really matured and developed during this period. We even began taking vacations together. I have a wonderful collection of photos from our various trips and will cherish them always. Mom was a lot of fun, and we understood each other. I loved being with her. She slowly shared her wisdom and strong recommendations for keeping one's business private. On occasion, we still had major differences of opinion and our strong wills would scratch at one another terribly. In the end, though, I recognized that she was most always right. I am so grateful that we had those good years together, enjoying life and each other's company. I wish it could have lasted longer—we had only eight more years after I became sober.

In the fall of 1993, although she had not smoked in more than twenty-five years, my mother was diagnosed with lung cancer. She was advised that the best course of treatment for her would be radiation at a hospital in Boston, so she came up from the Cape

and lived with me for about four months while under-
going the treatment.

One of the best memories I have of her during those
difficult days was when, right after one of her treatments,
she insisted that we go look for a dress for me because
I was going to a lavish wedding in Pasadena, California.
She knew that members of both the Kennedy and Shriver
families would be attending this one, and she wanted me
to look my very best. We went to the Vault section of
Boston's famous Filene's Basement, where they had a
vast collection of designer dresses. I pulled out a half
dozen dresses, which Mother quickly rejected. "They're
rags—put them back!" she asserted emphatically.

Amazingly, she started going through the racks
herself. Here she was scurrying around helping me right
after a horrific treatment that she later told me left her
throat feeling like scalding water had been poured down
it. "Ah," she finally exclaimed, "this is it!" She was
holding an exquisite, chocolate brown, layered sheath
dress with a sheer tulle top. "This will make a statement."
Was she ever right. The dress was drop-dead gorgeous!

When we finally got back home, my mother went
right upstairs to bed, saying that her throat and chest
were too sore for her to eat supper. She had kept going
all afternoon so I could have just the right dress. Later
on, she was happy when I attended the wedding with
Mark, and I wore the dress she had picked out for me,

knowing that I looked spectacular. She was an incredible woman and a real Alpha Chick.

Although my mother received extensive radiation for three months and was in remission, the cancer returned with a vengeance about two-and-a-half years later in the spring of 1996. This time she was dying. As the end of her life approached, we became even closer. On the night she later died, Mark drove me to the hospital, as I had an intuitive feeling she would be slipping away while I was there. He waited patiently outside as I went in to be with her and to say good-bye.

Mom and I held hands in her hospital room while oxygen was pumped into her weakened lungs. We were alone. The room was softly lit from the hallway. The only sound was the small beep on the respiration machine that represented my mother's heartbeat. I spoke to her quietly and told her it was OK to let go and for her not to worry—I would be fine. I told her I loved her dearly. I sensed that she was ready for the journey. I had taped a picture of my sister, my brother, and myself to her IV pole, and I took the picture down, folded it, and tucked it neatly into her hospital gown, telling her the photo would be going with her.

The beeps became slower and slower until they were a solid stream of humming, and she passed peacefully. Mom had prepared a living will in which she was very specific about not having tubes for feeding or resuscitation if her heart failed. She had been raised a Catholic and had exceptionally strong faith all her life. Perhaps because of this, she showed no fear of dying. She had the ability to make all of her own choices to the end, and to die, as she had lived, with dignity and grace.

A few months after my mother died, Scooter went on to win the three-year-old New England Morgan championship. Unfortunately, Mom didn't get to see how her suggestion that I get a hobby had reverberated in my life. Somehow, though, I think she knew that Scooter and I had both become winners.

My fiftieth birthday was marked by a quiet dinner with my family and Mark—no glam, no hats, no horns, and no champagne—just a lot of Perrier water. What a joy it was to sit across from my sister at dinner without watching her hold her breath, afraid of what I would do next!

The last thing I wanted at this time was a party. I liked waking up in the morning and knowing what I had done the night before. My life was almost everything I could dream of. I was at peace and no longer attached to my painful past. I had a beautiful home and a successful career. Scooter was the top three-year-old horse in New England, and Harley was my best little companion. I stood on a solid foundation of eight-and-a-half years of sobriety. Those days, I spent most of my spare time reading, listening to tapes, meditating, and getting to know who I really was. I was constantly working on self-improvement.

As for Mark, he had worked all his life as a manager in the restaurant his father owned. He had never worked anywhere else. When his father died, he lost his position at the restaurant as a result of inter-family litigation which he had devoted himself for almost forty years. Devastated, he eventually managed to get together enough money to open a restaurant of his own, and I jumped in to help him. While continuing to work full-time in my real estate business, I selected the decor and decorations for Mark's new venture. I spent quite a lot of my own money buying accessories to make the place look stylish and inviting. I worked, unpaid, as a hostess two or three evenings every week to help. One unseasonably warm Easter day, I even dressed up as the Easter Bunny with a huge plaster of Paris rabbit head and stood outside in the eighty-degree weather to bring in customers with their children!

I tried to help Mark remedy the runaway problems he began to have with staff, accounting, and inventory control. The truth is, he had never really managed the family restaurant where he had worked all those years. His father had done all the managing, and Mark had been mostly just a delightful and charming host. The customers loved him, but he really didn't know how to run a restaurant. He couldn't get tough with wait staff when they didn't show up on time or with cooks who ordered too much or the wrong food. I was certain the staff was stealing food and liquor.

To make things even worse, Mark's bookkeeper was coming to work drunk, writing vendor-payment checks in the wrong amount and not recording half of the checks she wrote; the books were a complete mess. His sons tried to point these things out to him, but Mark was too much of a nice guy to confront anyone about them. One day, I read him the riot act about the bookkeeper. I told him that he had to fire her and that if he didn't, I would. Well, I was the one who went in and told her she was fired because he just couldn't do it.

Looking back, I think that after working for so long under the reins of a strong-willed, controlling, vindictive father, Mark had lost whatever self-confidence he may have once had in his own ability to take control of a situation. His father had bought Mark his first home and his cars; he had called the shots. As with my own father and other men I had attracted into my life, I saw the pattern of "strong father, weak son" result in failure in the life of someone I cared for so very much. Mark's restaurant soon closed and he became a beaten man.

Because of this shift in his personality and his constant denial about the events and circumstances in his life, I knew I couldn't marry Mark or build a life with him. Eventually the romantic relationship was gone, but we became the best of friends. Neither of us had any false expectations about our relationship. The huge war Mark was having with his relatives over the family business and real estate was wearing him down, and he decided to move to Florida. We both felt that the best thing he could do for himself would be to get away from all of it and all of them. I was honestly happy for him and supported his decision. I was glad he was doing something for himself, and I was comfortable seeing him go.

My friendship with Mark, from the first time we met until his sudden and unexpected death after an operation, lasted ten years. The day he died, the universe lost a really good person. Through all the years, I had never heard him say a bad word about anyone. I returned with my new husband from my honeymoon on Nantucket to attend Mark's funeral, deeply saddened by his death.

During my relationship with Mark, I learned to develop appropriate boundaries for myself that reflected my newfound self-respect—no more emotional crumbs for me. My attitude about the way I expected a man to treat me had changed considerably. I expected honesty, accountability, integrity, and kindness—and my expectations were met.

With my new ability to love myself, I understood that men were the frosting on the cake, not the whole cake. My life, goals, and dreams were my cake, and I could make it any way I wanted—it was *my* recipe. Because I had come to realize that I was a complete human-being by myself, I also realized that a good man could add to my happiness, but he wouldn't be responsible for it. For the first time in my life, I was beginning to learn what a wonderful, loving, and supportive person I was. I know now that I am a great friend for someone to have, and that my loyalty is uncompromised. My Golden Rule is to try to always give a little more than what I get. Because I had developed genuine self-love, my life began to reflect that. What would my positive mental shift bring next?

Sweet Pea

For you to understand the next really significant series of events in my life, we need to go back to the year 1968, to the birth of a person who would become most dearly beloved and inspirational to me—another true Alpha Chick. On December 3, my sister Kathy called me to tell me that she had been coughing all day and was having stomach pains—she thought maybe she was getting a bug. The fact that she was nine months pregnant seems to have slipped her mind, but it was certainly on mine! I blurted out, "Do you think you're in labor?" She wasn't sure. I jumped into my car and drove frantically to her home in Needham, Massachusetts. When she opened the front door, she was hunched over holding her stomach. I knew then that she was in labor and panicked. When she told me she didn't know how to get to the hospital, I was really frightened, as I didn't either. Thank God I had left a note at home for my mother, who arrived ten minutes after me with her dear friend Marge. They immediately loaded my sister into their car, and off we went. Fortunately, Marge knew exactly how to get to Saint Margaret's Hospital in Dorchester.

I pulled in ahead of them, running into the hospital screaming that my sister was having a baby and for someone to get a stretcher. A large nun, dressed in an all-white habit, who had the neck and hands of a Muhammad Ali, pushed me into a chair. She strongly recommended that I settle down and said she would handle getting my sister checked in. Every time I got up to see what was happening, Sister Muhammad Ali glared me down. My sister was just about crowning when they wheeled her in. They had her upstairs and were prepping her for delivery while we frantically tried to find her husband, Phil, who was driving home from a business appointment at that time.

About an hour and a half later, Katherine Holly made her entrance into our lives. She was called Holly, a name I love, because she was born during the Christmas season. This beautiful little girl was to be my godchild, my "Sweet Pea," as I soon nicknamed her. This was the same year my relationship with Tony had ended, but Holly's joyous arrival made me forget about him for a while.

After a few days, mother and daughter were fine and able to go home. Holly was a beautiful, tiny infant with blond hair and enormous eyes. Our family now had its first grandchild and we were all very excited, especially my mother, who totally adored Holly from the moment she initially saw and held her.

Within the first few months of Holly's birth, my sister noticed that awful, unexplainable bruises began to appear on her daughter's body. I remember so clearly when she was about six months old and she had a little black eye—I figured she must have hit herself in the face. The bruises persisted, and sometime between Holly's first and second birthday, my sister took her for some medical testing. I can't remember how long it took to reach the diagnosis, I just remember hearing that my precious little Sweet Pea was a hemophiliac. Hemophilia is a rare bleeding disorder in which blood doesn't clot normally. Holly had less than one percent of the normal clotting factor. She would be prone to internal and external bleeding and bruising all of her life. Usually women are the carriers of this disease and their male children are the hemophiliacs. It is exceptionally rare for a woman to actually have the disease herself. Only one in 100 million women is a hemophiliac, while one in ten thousand men has the disease.[1]

During the next few years, our family learned about the complexities of Holly's illness and watched her go through several heartbreaking episodes requiring hospitalization. Without warning, she would develop internal bleeding in some part of her body. Starting when she was about five years old, her ankles were badly affected by internal bleeds. Without falling or stumbling or something traumatic that would appear to cause the problem occurring, one of her ankles would painfully swell and occasionally turn purple. We learned that what was happening was that blood from an internal bleed somewhere in a weak area of the leg would pool up in the joint of her ankle. The pain would become so distressing that she would limp and eventually be unable to walk at all. On these occasions, Kathy and Phil would take her to Tufts University's Floating Hospital for Children in Boston. There, fluid would be drained from her ankle and she would be given as many transfusions as necessary to replace her lost blood. At other times, Holly bled internally with only slight swelling, but always accompanied by gripping pain. Sometimes the internal bleeding showed up as blood in her urine or bowel movements, and sometimes she bled in an eye, which would then turn bright red.

Whenever these incidents occurred, Holly required hospitalization and transfusions. However, from the time she was a small child, Holly always displayed a very calm and courageous demeanor during her bleeding episodes. She never discussed what was happening with others.

She simply told her parents she needed "to go to the hospital," and she rarely cried as they drove her there. She usually had to stay in the hospital for several days until her condition stabilized.

Fluid drains, transfusions, in-patient hospital stays, and pain were things Holly had to endure her whole life. I still find it astonishing that she never complained or asked, "Why me?" She accepted her condition with fearlessness and showed an intense determination to live as fully as she could.

Holly's daily activities were restricted in an effort to eliminate threats to her health, which robbed her of some of the fun that more healthy people associate with childhood. She could not participate in sports. Special medications were always on hand. Her father told me that some of these injections cost thousands of dollars per shot. Both my sister and Holly became proficient at injecting her medicines. Holly always appeared cheerful, but was very private and protective about her medical condition. Except for her parents, and probably her brother and one very good friend, Holly never mentioned her illness or her health to anyone. She and I never once discussed it, and she didn't talk about it with my mother—they just had an understanding that Holly would tell Nana if she didn't feel well.

Despite her disability, Holly was a terrific kid with a wonderful personality. She was effervescent and enthusiastic. At the same time, she was a serious child and intellectually gifted. She spent a lot of time in her room reading and always went to do her homework when she arrived home from school each day. Like other girls, Holly played with dolls and had a dollhouse. She loved going to the Animal Rescue League summer day camp. She was a terrific conversationalist and wise beyond her years, and she conducted very adult conversations with the guests at her parents' frequent dinner parties. She was an adorable picture, a tiny girl with thick, curly blond hair, olive skin, and big, dark eyes. Everyone loved her.

When she was in middle school, Holly made friends with her classmate Sheila. Sheila was six foot one inch tall to Holly's four foot eleven; Sheila was the tallest child in the class, Holly the smallest. This classic Mutt-and-Jeff pair became fast friends; somehow they made each other comfortable. Perhaps their differences from their peers helped them to understand each other. Holly may have talked about her illness some with Sheila, and I'm certain she did with her younger brother Philip. She and her brother were very close all of their lives, and he had a profound understanding of the disappointments with which Holly had to live. However, I learned early on not to question her because I always got the same answer: "I'm fine." Most of the time, I limited my remarks to reassuring her that she was doing well. I respected the fact that she chose not to discuss it. Any information I received was usually secondhand, so I have pieced together the increasingly complex medical regimen she underwent throughout her life as best I can from memory.

When Holly was twelve, Sheila went with her to summer overnight camp for a month in New Hampshire and then went every summer for about five years. Holly was well enough to stay at camp for those summers and she loved it. She took all of her medicines with her and the counselors were familiarized with her special requirements and what to do in case of an emergency. Thank God she never had any major bleeding episodes while she was there. She had a couple of small incidents, and Kathy went up right away when these occurred. However, nothing happened that required Holly to be hospitalized or to leave camp.

During Holly's early teens, a medicine called recombinant factor IX was developed, which made a huge difference in her life, as it replaces the clotting factor which is missing from the blood of hemophiliacs. When she injected herself with factor IX, it would almost immediately stop a bleed. As a result of this new medicine, Holly's need for hospitalizations due to bleeding diminished. For a while, Holly was able to live a more normal life, and she became very involved in the camp. She became a counselor-in-training and eventually a counselor. She even interviewed girls who wanted to become campers. It was a great experience for her.

After factor IX became available, Holly ended up in the hospital only when she developed an infection. For example, if she got a bad cold and started coughing a lot, that could cause a bleed together with infection. She frequently had bloody noses. With all the health problems she had, though, to look at her, you would never have known how seriously ill she was—she had a gorgeous full head of blond hair, and in the summer, her skin became bronze.

My mother was very protective of her little grand-daughter—there was a special bond between them. Holly and her brother spent every summer at my parents' home in Cataumet on Cape Cod, and Holly always slept in Nana's room. You could hear Nana and Holly giggling and telling stories to one another every night. Nana took the children to yard sales, summer fairs, movies, and out for meals and ice cream. She taught them how to haggle over prices at yard sales—for example, if something was priced at one dollar, my mother would tell them to offer fifty cents. They received many a lesson at "Nana's School of Economics!" During the non-summer months, my mother would stay with Holly when her parents traveled. And of course she saw her on all the family holidays throughout the year. Whenever Holly had a bleeding episode or a hospitalization, my mother would reassure my sister that Holly would be just fine; she became a rock for Kathy to lean on. I know my mother was afraid for Holly and went to church to pray for her, but she never showed her fear around Kathy or Holly.

By her early teens, Holly had developed an enormous appetite for reading. It was her hobby and favorite pastime. I remember that while spending the summers with my mother on the Cape, she had stacks of books that she would whip through, reading two or three a week. Her avid reading also made her an excellent student. She decided that for high school she wanted to go to the Noble and Greenough School, where my father had gone, and she entered in her freshman year. Holly excelled in that academic environment. Amazingly, she also discovered a sport that was perfect for her, and she became captain of the girls' golf team. This adorable, tiny young woman had a killer golf swing, and she addressed the ball with perfection. I played with her several times over the years, and watching her swing her "Big Bertha" is one of my fondest memories. I would hear that perfect *ping* sound and her drive would fly straight out—I wondered how she did it. This was so typical of Holly. Everything she undertook, she did with excellence. She refused to let her illness hold her back.

As Holly grew up, I loved to take her to the movies and ice shows, and also shopping—early on for toys and then later for clothes. We got along beautifully and truly enjoyed each other's company. I wanted Holly to have some fun in her life, and there was nothing I would not do for her. Although my gifts of clothing and jewelry may have been excessive, I just couldn't help myself—there was already too much that she couldn't have and would never have. I wanted her to have everything her heart desired that I was capable of giving her, especially because I knew that although she experienced very tough times with her illness, she never showed it.

When we went shopping for clothes, we usually laughed ourselves silly. Holly knew exactly what she wanted to wear and she loved fine clothing. I'm sure she inherited her good taste from my mother and her own mother because they both were really elegant dressers. Over the years, due to her various medications, Holly's wardrobe became more challenging as her body proportions changed dramatically. (She went from being painfully thin to developing a large area of fat around her waist.) She loved Chinese food, and we always finished our shopping expeditions with a great dinner at a Chinese restaurant.

On June 3, 1987, Holly graduated with honors from Noble and Greenough, with plans to enter the nursing program at Georgetown University in Washington, D.C. in the fall. My graduation gift to her was a trip to Paris with me—just the two of us in the most beautiful city in the world! I'm sure my sister was ready to tear her hair out when she imagined all the dreadful things that could go wrong if I were drinking while Holly was traveling with me. Reluctantly, however, Kathy gave her approval. Although I was still actively drinking, I knew I would never do anything to put Holly at risk.

We had to carry special injections of factor IX with us in case Holly needed them for an emergency. Traveling internationally with vials of medicine and syringes is pretty complicated. We had to have doctors' letters of explanation in order to get permission to take her medical supplies into France.

Nevertheless, our vacation together was glorious. Although the Parisian weather was on the cool side for the month of June, it didn't hinder us from extensive sightseeing, shopping at the best boutiques, and indulging in extravagant fine dining in the evenings. Through a friend, the head of Data General Corporation, I had arranged a connection for us with the top Data General executive in Paris. His name was Jean Pierre, and he gave us a royal tour of the Parisian nightlife. We went to the legendary Harry's New York Bar and all the best discos. I took endless pictures, and in every one Holly is beaming with her huge smile. I did everything I could short of standing on my head under the Eiffel Tower to make her laugh. Since most of the time she lived with so many restrictions, I wanted this trip to be one Holly would never forget. I know she had a wonderful time, and she had no medical problems. Thinking of our trip today makes me very sad—I wish I had had more times with her like those we had in Paris.

Tiny and immaculately groomed, Holly went off to college. She loved Georgetown, which had been her first-choice college, and her freshman year was uneventful. Unfortunately, however, her sophomore year started off with a horrific accident. She was hit by a car while crossing a street near campus. The poor man who hit her ended up driving her back to her dorm. Although Holly initially thought she was going to be all right, her injuries actually caused very complicated internal bleeding and she ended up in the hospital. Her parents flew to Washington immediately, and I got down on my knees nightly and prayed for her recovery. Surely God was with her, because, blessedly, she pulled through after a few weeks of hospitalization followed by a few more weeks of bed rest. Of course, Holly kept her books with her and insisted on staying at school. Fortunately, a dear family friend who lived in Washington watched over her closely while she recovered. Holly never missed turning in a paper or completing a test during this time. She did not allow her illness to interfere with her studies. Her grades were consistently in the highest of her class and she eventually graduated with honors.

Shortly after this life-threatening accident, the doctors told Holly that she had developed a grave complication. Like most hemophiliacs, she had required countless blood transfusions over the years to offset the blood she lost. Until 1992, blood transfusions were not screened for illnesses as they are today before being given to a patient. Holly learned she had been infected by HIV (human immunodeficiency virus) from one of her transfusions.

Because of factor IX, she had been able to manage her hemophilia fairly successfully for fourteen years, and were it not for the HIV she might have been able to live a relatively normal life for years to come. But HIV changed all of that. Now, in addition to the injections, she had to take the HIV "cocktail." Her medication regimen became extremely complex and involved taking from twenty to thirty pills several times a day. She also had to take some liquid medicines which she mixed in juice every morning. I remember noticing her bureau at my mother's house on the Cape one day. I looked at all the pills and paraphernalia that were laid out on top of it and thought, *Oh, my God—this child has to take all this medicine every day!* I was completely overwhelmed by what I had seen and the realization of what Holly had to do just to keep herself alive. She would have to take all this medicine every day for the rest of her life, and she wasn't yet twenty-one years old. Amazing us all once again, she adjusted to these changes and managed every detail without a complaint.

When Holly was diagnosed with HIV, Kathy asked me not to tell our mother. She thought it would be more than Mom could handle, and I agreed. So Nana never knew that Holly had contracted HIV for, of course, Holly never talked about it, and Mom never did have to know when Holly's illness declined further because Mom had passed away by then.

During the summer that followed her sophomore year, Holly became withdrawn and almost reclusive for a while. I think any hope she may have had of living a potentially normal life had been shattered by the HIV diagnosis. She had always loved to visit my mother's house on the Cape, and that summer I watched her sit on the veranda watching the ocean for hours. I believed she was daydreaming. I like to think that in those daydreams she was able to live her life the way she wished it could have been: getting married, having children, dancing . . . enjoying a full life. Sadly, I think she also must have spent some of that time thinking about how she was going to die and processing that painful reality.

Holly's health had become a vicious roller-coaster ride. She bounced back and forth from relatively uneventful daily living to struggling with the effects of her severely compromised immune system. There were good days followed by bad days, and she never knew which she would have. Holly did not complain as the boundaries of her world became smaller and smaller.

More and more limitations were put on her activities and travel plans because she was so susceptible to catching the flu and colds, which would hospitalize her.

Holly graduated with honors from Georgetown's nursing program in 1991. However, due to her HIV, she would not be able to use her education to care for patients. After all the work she had done at Georgetown, having the opportunity to use her nursing education taken away so abruptly must have been another huge disappointment. Yet she never discussed it. Actually, none of us did. My heart ached for her.

From 1992 through 1999, Holly experienced bouts of severe illness, which would be followed by a year or so of reasonable health. We never knew how long the good times would last before she would be stricken again by some complication related to her hemophilia or HIV.

When she was well enough, Holly assisted her mother with her real estate business, helping to show multi-million-dollar homes. She would appear impeccably dressed in a fabulous suit, knowing every intricate detail of the property. The buyers' brokers were in awe of her knowledge and professionalism. As always, in true Holly style, she would do her absolute best and not let her illnesses hold her down. She also assisted in interviewing prospective students for Georgetown University.

Despite the devastating circumstances of her health, Holly entered Boston College Law School in the fall of

1999. Her dream was now to become a child advocate, and she was feeling very optimistic. She wanted to combine her medical knowledge with the law to help children. The HIV was under control for the time being and she was experiencing a period of good health, which for Holly meant no sudden hospitalizations due to a catastrophic bleeding episode or a life-threatening infection.

Holly loved law school and relished the apprentice work she did for some of the largest law firms in Boston. She represented immigrants in the Boston area, resolving housing issues. Her focus was always on those less fortunate than herself. She may have been petite in stature, but Holly was a giant mentally and a master of negotiation. For years, my sister had put her in charge of returning anything she needed to take back to a store; by the time she was finished with her negotiating spiel, the contrite company would be begging Holly to let them take back the goods and give her an exchange! We all marveled at her skill. There seemed no limitations on what she could accomplish with her gifted and compelling arguments, just perfect for a future child advocate.

In the summer of 2000, the Major League Baseball All-Star Game was being held in Boston. Holly was in a window of good health, and I asked her what she would like to do most. Without one second of hesitation she responded, "It would be amazing to see the All-Star Game." The game had been a sellout for months, but I prayed to God to find me two tickets. I started calling ticket agencies, and a person at one of them recommended an outfit in New Hampshire. He said if anyone had a ticket it would be this place. I called them, and indeed they had two spectacular seats in the second row next to the Red Sox dugout. I never gave any consideration to what the price might be, which turned out to be $5,000 for the two tickets! But I was so grateful I was able to buy them—it was worth every penny and more to be with Holly at this game.

We truly had a wonderful time. Holly was able to see many of the legendary players who were all around us, including Ted Williams, who sat just in front of us with his son. As an added bonus, Kevin Costner was on the field about twenty feet away from us. I was yelling hello to him as if I knew him, and Holly laughed hysterically when he turned and waved at us. Then I pretended to climb up on the dugout to see the players, and she grabbed my arm to pull me back. She was laughing so hard she got tears in her eyes. I could never put a price on the joy I felt at seeing Holly in such high spirits that evening—she had a deliriously happy experience. This was the way I had hoped her life would always be.

I thank God for the opportunity I was given to have times like this with Holly. That day we talked about taking a trip to China to see the Great Wall. We were both fascinated by that area of the world and its people. At that moment, going to the Far East seemed like a real possibility. I could not have imagined that my time with Holly would be coming to an end all too soon.

Sometime after receiving the news of her HIV diagnosis, Holly began to attend a Catholic church in Boston called the Urban Center, which was attended by many people from Boston's gay community. Its parishioners included a huge number of HIV patients who were very involved in church activities. Holly loved the Urban Center and felt at home there—she could express her spirituality in a safe and welcoming place where she wasn't "different." Her parents attended Mass with her there instead of going to their church in the suburbs.

Father George was rector of the church. He and Holly became very close, and I believe he was her confessor. Father George was an extraordinarily gifted priest, also serving as the chaplain of Boston's Brigham and Women's Hospital. I believe he was sent into Holly's life to help her through these most difficult times. My family loved him for his unique ministry. I admired and respected him so much that later on I asked him to officiate at my wedding ceremony. Sadly, in 2007, the Archdiocese of Boston closed the Urban Center, which had offered such an important ministry to Boston's gay and HIV communities. Fortunately, though, it was there for Holly when she needed it.

Just as Holly had begun to adjust to the HIV treatment regimen and was regaining some balance in her life, in the fall of 2000 her liver began to fail. She had contracted another illness, the contagious liver disease hepatitis C, most likely from another unscreened blood transfusion. Her immune system was so compromised by all the infections and the HIV that she had little resistance to this new disease.

(Sadly, most hemophiliacs who were given transfusions in the 1980s and early '90s have lost their personal battles with HIV and/or hepatitis C. These additional infections from contaminated blood became so prevalent that in 1998, the Ricky Ray Hemophilia Relief Fund was authorized by Congress. This fund was named after a young teenager from Florida who had been infected with HIV from tainted blood products and died in 1992. Katherine Muir, then National Hemophilia Foundation president, thanked President Clinton for signing the legislation, which compensates victims of unscreened blood products or their families. At the time that he signed the bill, twenty-six other countries had already created such funds.[2])

Now that Holly was battling three life-threatening illnesses—hepatitis C, hemophilia, and HIV—her hospitalizations became more frequent. It was so horrible and felt so unfair. Our great fear was always that she would develop pneumonia and die. Her body had also become resistant to antibiotics used to treat pneumonia. She had been given so many megadoses that they were ceasing to be effective. Every good day at this point was a miracle.

Holly was now subjected to some exceptionally painful and invasive procedures. These included frequent endoscopies, during which a tube with a camera on the end was inserted from her mouth into her stomach to check for internal bleeding, usually because she had been vomiting blood. Her medical regimen was augmented to include daily injections of the powerful and expensive drug interferon, the effects of which were like having a chemotherapy treatment daily. The cost of these medications was many thousands of dollars per injection. Her family was fortunate to have had excellent medical insurance to cover most of the costs. The drug ravaged her body—she lost all the fat from her face, arms, and legs, and her hair fell out.

Despite her appearance and how sick she felt, however, Holly continued to attend her law school classes. She wouldn't let the new treatments stop her. When her law books became too heavy for her to carry, I bought her a fashionable bag on wheels to help her maneuver them. I don't know how she did it, but she managed to finish her second year of law school, although she ended up taking exams later than the rest of the students due to her hospitalizations.

During the summer break, Holly's health slipped a little each day. I called her often to see how she was doing and she always answered, "I'm fine." She never gave even the slightest indication that anything was wrong. I still wonder how she mustered the courage every day to make her family think she was all right when she knew inside that she was dying. I am certain she wanted to spare us. Rather than feeling sorry for herself, Holly was worried about us. Where did she get the strength to endure?

It is still so painful for me to think about what happened to Holly. First it was the hemophilia, which robbed her of so much of her childhood. Then factor IX came along and gave her life back to her for a few years. Were it not for the contaminated transfusions, Holly might have been able to live a relatively healthy and happy life. The few good years she did have were probably a gift; she surely made the most of every moment. But suddenly she was hit with her HIV diagnosis, with all of its debilitating effects and complications. And just when she had learned to manage the medications and live with this new disease, she was brought down once more by the hepatitis C virus, destroying any lingering hope she may have had. I cannot imagine the strength it took for Holly to cope with all of these conditions, but I do know that through it all she had a very strong faith in God, like her mother and grandmother—they were all devout Catholics. Maybe it was her faith that enabled her to be so courageous when she received what she knew was essentially a death sentence.

From the time Holly was a little girl until she was thirty-two years old, her parents dedicated their lives to her care. She was their primary focus. Though Kathy and Phil knew that Holly's health continued to worsen, I don't think they realized quite how grave the situation was that summer. Still, Kathy was beside herself. She told me she knew Holly wasn't well and that Holly did not want to talk about her deteriorating condition even to her mother. She remained an extraordinarily private person right until the end. I later learned from Dr. Mark Klempner, the HIV specialist who cared for Holly for many years, that she was very aware of her situation. She knew she was dying. She had done her own research and knew full well the prognosis for a hepatitis-C patient with a compromised immune system. Nevertheless, she resumed her third year of law school classes in the fall of 2001.

On Saturday, November 10, my sister called to say that she and Phil needed to go to a business function and Holly was going to be alone at home. None of us wanted her to be alone for the evening so I said I'd come down and take her out for a little dinner. I talked with Holly on the phone and she seemed eager to go out. I hadn't seen her for several weeks because of school, and when I picked her up I was shocked by her appearance and weakness. She could barely climb into my SUV, which was just slightly higher off the ground than a regular car. My Sweet Pea was so thin. Her face was skeletal. Her skin had developed a yellowish tinge, and even the whites of her eyes were discolored. I had to bite my lip to prevent myself from crying.

I felt as though there was a dagger in my heart as we drove to the restaurant. Because she could no longer digest proteins or eat sugar or salt, finding food she could eat had become very difficult and complicated. I came up with the idea that we should order lots of little dishes, saying that it would be fun to sample this or that. What I was really thinking was that this way she could pick at what might be palatable for her. Thoughts about Holly and her dire situation swirled in my head throughout our meal. I could see that she was dying. I could barely swallow because the lump in my throat was choking me. How could this be happening?

The fact is that Holly had tried to hide the progression of her hepatitis C from all of us for as long as she could, but because of the HIV, her body had no ability to resist its hideous effects. Now that she was in the final stage of liver failure, she could no longer hide her condition. I must have seemed crazy to the people at the tables around us because I was trying so hard to make her laugh. I noticed people staring a bit because she looked so sick. However, Holly acted as if she was unaware of the attention her appearance was attracting.

As we drove home my heart was sinking, but I forced myself to keep the conversation going. I did not want her to know that I realized how sick she was. I helped her from the car and went inside with her. I hugged her and held her close; her dear body felt so small in my arms. I could tell she was exhausted. I left, telling her I would talk to her the next day. I got in my car and the first thing I did was call her mother's cell phone. Kathy answered and I shared with her how sick I thought Holly seemed. I kept saying, "She is in trouble. She is in trouble." My sister sadly agreed but said Holly had continued to say she was OK.

Holly rallied and went to school the following Monday, Tuesday, and Wednesday. However, on Thursday she could not get out of bed, and Kathy immediately called Dr. Klempner. This man had given Holly the most compassionate and excellent medical treatment for the previous nine years. Through his genius and experiments with various cutting-edge medicines, he had probably extended her life to this point.

On Friday morning, Kathy and Phil took Holly to the hospital. As they pushed her into the hospital in a wheelchair, Dr. Klempner was waiting. He looked at Holly and then at my sister, shaking his head slightly from side to side—there was nothing more he could do for her. He told Kathy and Phil that Holly's journey was coming to an end and that she had very little time left.

My sister called me later to tell me this news. I was at a gift show, looking for a bracelet to buy Holly for Christmas. I dropped the jewelry, ran out the door, and stood trembling in the parking lot. Then I tried to drive, but I was crying so hard that I couldn't see where I was going. I had to pull over to the side of the road, slumping over the steering wheel as I sobbed uncontrollably. How was I going to pull myself together for Holly's sake and for the family?

Because she was dehydrated, Holly was admitted to the hospital for fluid infusions. While Kathy and Phil were spending the day with her there, they called her brother, who was living in New York, and told him it was time to come say good-bye to Holly. Kathy recommended that I go see her the next day in the hospital before they took her home on Sunday; there was nothing more to do except keep her comfortable.

At this point, my poor sister had to start thinking about making funeral arrangements. I honestly do not know how she was able to do this. It must have been the strong Irish temperament she inherited from my mother, together with her lifelong faith, that gave her the strength she needed.

On Saturday evening, I went to the hospital and found Holly sitting comfortably in her bed. Her large brown eyes were pensive and at times she looked off. I like to think that she was seeing her grandmother reaching out for her. I talked to her about the Great Wall of China again and the possibly of our going there together. She looked right at me and said, "Mal, I won't be making this trip with you"—she was telling me she was dying. I told her she should just hold on to the thought that we might go and not give up yet.

I knew this might be the last time I would be able to talk to Holly, so I told her how proud I was of her, how much I loved her, and that I had always felt like she was my daughter, too. (Interestingly, the difference in our height aside, in many ways we resembled one another.) I could see that she was at peace with what was happening to her. She had given every ounce of her strength to fight this long battle, and now she had surrendered. She knew the end was near and she wasn't afraid. Her parents returned with her brother. I knew that every minute they could be together with Holly was crucial, so I hugged and kissed her and told her I would see her the next day at home.

Kathy and Phil didn't want Holly to die in the sterility of the hospital, but rather in her own bed in her own room, surrounded by the people who loved her. I asked Kathy what I could do to help, and she gave me a long list of medical supply items the hospital had told her would be needed when they took Holly home. My brother Larry and I drove around to medical supply companies and drugstores all that evening to make sure we got everything on the list, and we took the supplies to the house that night. None of them would be needed or used.

The next morning around 11:30, the ambulance backed into the driveway of their house. The back doors opened and I watched as the EMTs lifted Holly out in a chair-type stretcher. Her small head was rolling from side to side and she was making slight little moans. She was slipping into a coma. The tears were rolling down my face as they took her through the front door. My sister followed them with her hand on Holly's shoulder.

Dear God, don't let me fall down and cause a scene, I prayed silently, because I was feeling my knees give way. The grief that I was feeling was actually knocking me off my feet. I know today that if I had not had my sobriety, I never would have gotten through this in any coherent way. I immediately would have tried to kill the pain I was feeling with alcohol, and who knows how long I would have remained drunk. Sobriety has enabled me to be there for the people I love when they need me.

The hospice nurse got Holly into bed and made sure she was comfortable. I knelt on the floor next to her and held her hand, and we had a few minutes alone together. Although she wasn't able to respond, I told her I wished there was something more I could have done. I told her I would have given my life for hers. I know without any doubt that she knew how much I loved her. Finally, I said, "Nana is waiting for you. She's going to be right there with you. There is nothing to fear."

The whole family gathered around Holly's bed in her beautiful sun-filled room. There were stephanotis orchids in perfect bloom on her desk. Her mother and brother were on either side of Holly on top of the bedcovers. Her dad was close by, and her grandmother Aily, with whom she also had a wonderful and loving bond, sat in a chair at her left side. At this moment, I almost felt it was a blessing that my mother had died five years earlier. If she had been there, seeing Holly like this would have killed her on the spot. Although she had always been so strong, Mom would not have been able to endure this. Holly's uncle Larry (my brother), and two very dear friends who had introduced Holly to the Urban Center. Holly's priest, Father George, was at her side, and her beloved dog, Kerry, was at the foot of her bed. Holly was surrounded by love on a beautiful New England fall afternoon. God had given us all the gift of having her at home with her family once more.

I watched Holly take her last few breaths. She was in a coma, but her eyes were open. We were all telling Holly how much we loved her, and there were a couple of little tears in the corners of her eyes. She never moved or flinched, and she had such a peaceful look on her face—it was almost like a smile. I really believe that she was seeing

a light and also my mother. I know my mother was there—
she loved that child so very deeply. Holly died peacefully
at approximately two o'clock. As I was writing about her
for this book, I could hardly see what I was typing because
my eyes were filled with tears. It seemed like she had died
only recently, but many years had already gone by.

A few hours after Holly passed away, her brother
went into the basement of their home and started
working on a mosaic mural. This was his way to process
his grief. He had become a very accomplished artist and
was recognized for his work with mosaic tiles and their
intricate details. He cut miniscule pieces of tile and
placed them in a picture frame. He created a small red
sailboat tossed about by a huge storm in a cold gray sea;
the little boat remained afloat while surrounded by
threatening whitecaps. At the top of the picture were the
words "Courage to Endure." I cannot think of three
words that describe more perfectly Holly's life and her
challenges. My sister has the original picture, which is
approximately forty-eight by sixty inches, in her home.
It is a masterpiece, like Holly's life.

Holly's funeral was held four days later in the
Boston College Law School chapel. A police detail on
Harley Davidson motorcycles with sirens roaring
escorted us through the campus to the front of the
church. Holly's dad knew she would have loved those
bikes for she always commented on them, and he

arranged this private detail for the funeral procession. The church was filled to capacity with people who loved her. Holly, this petite and courageous woman, had touched so many lives in infinite ways.

The eulogies described the courage and determination which had carried Holly through the enormous medical battles she had experienced. Dr. Klempner gave an extraordinary talk about her, sharing with us the enormity of her medical treatment. He explained that at various times she was on four intravenous and oral medicines for the hemophilia. She took twelve different medications for the HIV infection, as well as an experimental drug. She took twenty different antibiotics to treat infections that her immune system could not ward off. And she had multiple insulin injections and finger sticks for sugar measurements daily. In addition, she used inhalers for her weakened lungs and required four other injections for the hepatitis C. He told us that this was the most complex medical situation he had ever dealt with in his long career.

Holly's father and her cousin Miles and I also spoke of her endless courage to endure and her drive to go on, and her dear friend from grade school days, Sheila, read a poem Holly had written long before when they were at camp together. The funeral was an extraordinary tribute to Holly's life, accomplishments, and the glory of the human spirit. Her essence in the church was tangible.

I know that practicing the five steps of the Alpha Chick process, which you will learn more about in Part Two, helped me to be able to handle Holly's death. As I worked through them on that last morning with her, I realized that she was ready and had accepted her fate. Her body could not go on, but her mind was at peace. Nevertheless, a few days after her funeral, I started to unravel. I was overtaken by sudden bouts of uncontrollable crying. Again, I sat quietly and started to rethink her passing. Many of the things Holly had said to me over the past several months replayed in my mind. There had been a message in them that I hadn't been able to hear when she was talking to me. She had suggested many times in a very obscure way that there was no future for her.

I've told my husband Michael several times in the past few years that I still have to make the trip to the Great Wall of China. He understands my need to fulfill the joint dream Holly and I shared. I told her we would go to China together, and I am determined to keep my promise. When I stand in front of that wall, I know she will be there with me.

When I think of Holly, I imagine the soaring possibilities of the spirit of a true Alpha Chick. Holly was born one and showed it in the way she lived every day of her life. This poem from her personal journal reveals her simple but powerful plea for God's guidance:

Pray a lot
Overlook a lot
And improve a little each day
God help me to live that

Every day, even now, during my meditation, I send my love to Holly. Some nights I go outside looking for a shining star in the sky, knowing she will be there. I wave and wipe my tears away. Holly, my Sweet Pea, you will always be with me. You have inspired my life and this book, and you will live on in my heart and in these pages.

Dr. Delicious

Now that I've shared with you the stories of my mother and Holly, two Alpha Chicks who were such inspirational and beloved role models for me, I want to introduce you to the other most important person in my life. But first I need to give you a little history prior to and leading up to his entry into my world.

After Mark moved to Florida, I was on my own once more, but something was different this time. Being single really didn't faze me— I no longer needed a man to complete my identity. I went on weekend retreats with Harley and loved every minute by myself. I also traveled alone to international vacation spots and went whenever and wherever I wanted to go. I enjoyed my freedom.

One memorable trip was when I flew to England by myself and met up with a group of tennis enthusiasts going to Wimbledon. It so happened that a *Sports Illustrated* reporter, who specialized in women's tennis and lived near me, had just left for England to cover the Wimbledon matches. She had gotten my name from a friend and contacted me to ask if I would be willing to bring her laptop computer to England, as she had inadvertently left it behind. I had already planned my trip, was happy to help, and of course agreed and delivered it to her as soon as I arrived. The reporter was so appreciative that she gave me press seats at center court for the women's final between Serena and Venus, (the Williams sisters), in which they played against one another in a finals match for the very first time! She also took me into the players' pavilion to meet the Williams sisters and some of the other contenders. It was a fabulous trip and I enjoyed every minute of it.

On another vacation, I traveled by myself to Hawaii for a real estate association conference at which Jack Canfield, author of *Chicken Soup for the Soul*, was the featured speaker. I had the opportunity to talk with him at length about his book and his ideas about positive thinking and self-motivation. It was a rich experience. And, of course, Hawaii was gorgeous and a wonderful place for a business vacation.

I loved traveling alone. I always met fascinating people, took interesting photos, and was never restricted by another's schedule. My happiness was my own.

After about a year, I thought I might enjoy dating again, and some friends suggested I try online dating and told me about Match.com. At first I was very resistant to the idea of meeting anyone that way. God forbid if my sister found out—she would think I was really desperate and worry that I would meet Jack the Ripper, and I'm not sure which she would have thought was worse! Kathy's personality is like my mother's in that she is a very private person. She never discusses personal family business and would be mortified if she had to admit we were related if I did anything she would consider embarrassing, which in the past included just about everything I ever did. I, on the other hand, am more like my dad—I inherited his easygoing nature. In sobriety I have remained adventurous, and am not afraid of taking chances if I think the results will be good for me. However, I thankfully no longer put myself in dangerous or life-threatening situations.

So I began to dabble cautiously with online dating, screening people and responding with brief e-mails, including more questions than you'd find on a credit application. It was like shopping in a huge supermarket. I was very careful, met my dates in public places to which I drove myself, and always let someone know where I was going, whom I was meeting, and when to expect me home. Using these techniques, I met some really nice people. The men I met via online dating were very refreshing—more mature, respectful, and successful than the men I'd previously met in bars after a few drinks.

In my online description of myself, I stated that I was a successful professional and that my career was very important to me. I said that I owned my own home, loved to travel, was very independent, and had a dog who slept at the foot of my bed! The responses I received were from an array of professional men who weren't interested in meeting women in bars. All of them had fulfilling and demanding careers and, like me, were using online dating as a way to meet people in a nonthreatening environment in which they could screen them and ask questions. I was able to develop a commonality in these pre-meeting communications, which was a lot safer than encountering the kinds of people I'd met with my girlfriends in Boston bars. I had been down that path before—it would have been like driving my car in reverse.

I communicated only with people who included a photograph in their online profile. I didn't want to end up meeting someone who might misrepresent himself. A few years earlier, a realtor friend had told me she met some fabulous men through the personals section of *Boston Magazine*. I answered a few of the magazine's personal ads, but unfortunately they did not include pictures. I had an exchange of correspondence with a fellow from a nearby town, a very articulate man who described himself as tall, handsome, charming, and financially solvent. So I agreed to meet him at Finally Michael's restaurant in Framingham.

When I arrived, I stood at the entrance of the restaurant looking around for someone who was tall, handsome, and charming, as he had described himself, and I didn't see anyone who fit that description. However, there was a short, sweaty-looking man in front of me with a toupee that looked like roadkill. I said to myself, *Please, dear God, this can't be the man.* He had said he was tall and good-looking, and I thought, *You've got to be kidding.* What was that thing on his head? Holy mackerel—you could have scrubbed windows with it!

I was almost speechless, but I managed to say to him, "You're John?" When the man said he was, I replied, "I think you might have misrepresented yourself a little bit. You said you were tall and good-looking. I don't think you're tall—you're not even close to my height." (Believe me, I could have added a lot more, but I didn't.) Then I said, "You know what? I'm going to have a glass of water and then I'm going to leave." And that's what I did.

Please don't misunderstand and think that looks are the only important thing to me when it comes to a man. Rather, I was annoyed by his dishonesty. At that point in my life, honesty was what I wanted most. If his ad had said, "I'm kind, friendly, with a great sense of humor, and if looks don't matter to you, I'm your guy," or anything remotely honest, I probably wouldn't have walked out the way I did. But "tall and good-looking" was just too much. The next day I called up my friend and said vehemently, "Don't ever tell me to try the personals in *Boston Magazine* again!"

Match.com was much better because you could see what the person looked liked. Through this service I met and dated a terrific man I will call Fred, an executive at a technology company and a recent widower. He was truly a wonderful human being and became a good friend. Fred was very respectful of the fact that I did not drink, although he himself had an occasional cocktail. He was extremely sports-oriented, and he got me back into skiing and playing golf. We had great fun together.

Fred lived in the wilds of a small New England town, and I called him "Mr. Greenjeans." He could get up on a Sunday morning and roller skate several miles of shoreline near where he lived, then skate all the way back. Next, he'd want to play eighteen holes of golf. After that he'd say, "Maybe we should go play tennis." I'd reply, "I don't think so—I'm about ready to have a heat stroke!"

As lovely a person as Fred was, there were some major disconnects between us, and I began to understand that he wasn't the one for me. He wanted somebody who would like living in the woods, going to Little League games to watch his grandchildren, baking apple pies, and wearing Birkenstocks. But I'm a city girl. I don't make pies, I'm not interested in Little League, and I like fancy clothes and designer shoes like Manolo Blahniks.

Also, Fred almost never maintained the things he owned. His house was in need of repair, his clothing was worn and faded, and his car looked like it had been the poor loser in a demolition derby—sometimes it even got stuck in reverse.

All these things drove me crazy. I do like a man who can look elegant when the occasion calls for it, and taking care of my house and car are important to me. I know these qualities aren't what make a good person, but they surely influence lifelong relationships. I knew I could never adapt to Fred's lifestyle, nor he to mine. Yet Fred was a good and loyal friend, and he was always extremely nice to me. He was there for me when Holly died, and came to the funeral. He was present in a loving and kindhearted way, and I appreciated that so very much.

I have heard it said that when you have a huge void in your life, God will fill it. I believe that is how "Dr. Delicious" ended up on my computer screen. About a month after Holly's death, I received an e-mail from a man who had read my online bio and was interested in meeting me. At that time, I was just barely surviving Holly's loss, and I quickly responded that I was grieving the loss of my niece and not scheduling social activities. He understood and sent me a few follow-up e-mails about the grieving process. After a few more exchanges, he and I discovered that we had a mutual friend in real estate and AA. We decided to meet for lunch before I left for the Christmas holiday with my sister and the rest of the family; we all needed to go someplace where we could try to get through Christmas without Holly, and skiing in Vermont seemed like a reasonable choice.

I met Dr. Michael Pearlman at the Cheesecake Factory in the Atrium Mall in Chestnut Hill on December 23, 2001. He was fifty-nine years old, five years older than I was. He was also a nondrinker and had his own history with alcohol, which immediately made me more comfortable. When this man first walked in, I was pleasantly surprised by how attractive he was—the online photos had not captured his good looks. He was definitely tall, and elegantly dressed in a dark-blue cashmere topcoat, with an open-necked, bright-blue dress shirt. The shirt made his sparkling blue eyes and beautiful, thick, sandy-blond hair really stand out. Approaching the table, he had a genuine smile and appeared to like what he was seeing when spotting me.

Michael was charming. He had a wonderful sense of humor and seemed at ease with himself. He wasn't a bit pretentious. He ordered a fire-roasted artichoke, something I happen to like quite a lot too, but which was definitely not a typical restaurant selection for most men I'd known. As he pulled the leaves off the artichoke, I noticed how well kept his hands were. I listened closely as he spoke enthusiastically about his work and children.

While Michael talked, I couldn't help but think about all the qualities I had put on my list that the perfect man for me would have. I had written that he would be a little over six feet tall and beautifully groomed—someone who took care of himself. I described a solid professional who was financially independent, with a good sense of humor and with whom I would feel comfortable. Also, not drinking was a plus. Michael seemed to have them all! I was quietly impressed that we were off to such a good start.

Volumes have been written about the elusive chemical reactions that make men and women attractive to each other, and I am by no means an expert on any of that stuff. I only know that I found Michael very appealing, and I'm sure he could tell I was interested. I thought he was attracted to me as well. Whether chemistry is part looks, part pheromones, part common interests, and/or part spiritual connection, who knows? But whatever it is, I knew for sure it was going on between us. This kind of connection was very different from what I had experienced with men I'd met in bars. For one thing, neither of us was under the influence of any drug or alcohol that enhanced, exaggerated, or numbed our real feelings and perceptions. We knew exactly what we were seeing and experiencing, and it felt good. We were both comfortable and enjoying our conversation during the meal.

After lunch, we strolled around the mall chatting as I picked up a few things for my holiday ski trip, and we agreed to meet again in the new year. As I drove home from our lunch date, my cell phone rang. It was Michael, calling to let me know that he thought I was "absolutely perfect." Quite a compliment after a first date! This was his way of letting me know he enjoyed meeting me and reassuring me that the pain I was feeling as a result of Holly's death was perfectly natural. Several days later, he left me a short voice mail, checking to see how I was holding up through the holiday. I did not have cell service, so I could not return the call. However, I was impressed by his thoughtfulness and his caring, which seemed totally genuine. This was a "real person" I had met.

In Vermont, I skied at Sugarbush Mountain aggressively every day, trying to exhaust myself. Being outdoors and busy made the time pass more quickly—that is, until I had a horrific fall and broke my arm! I was skiing well with one of the pros from the mountain when I suddenly did a face plant in the snow. For twenty minutes facedown I waited for the emergency ski patrol to come and help scrape me up. The pain was so intense that I could only see little points of light, no color whatsoever. They took me to the emergency medical clinic at the base of the mountain, where they confirmed I had broken one of the bones in my left arm.

For the next few days I was in the most excruciating pain I have ever experienced, so bad that I had to be heavily medicated to get through it. What a nightmare! My arm was one solid, dark purple bruise from my shoulder to the ends of my fingers, and swollen to twice its usual size—I was a mess. I did not want to spoil everyone's trip by returning home early, so I just stayed in bed for the next four days until it was time to go back.

Worst of all, I had broken my *left* arm and I am *very* left-handed. My sister pleaded with me to come and stay with her—she was convinced that I would not be able to manage with one arm—but I didn't want to do this. I wanted to be in my own home, in familiar surroundings with my dog. I promised I'd call her if I ran into trouble, but I was determined to take care of Harley and myself. I didn't want anyone taking care of me and telling me what to do to get better.

The orthopedic surgeon I saw in Boston the day after I got back told me that my arm would have to remain immobilized for the next six weeks. He said that I wouldn't be able to shower for the next several days, but I could take a bath if I kept my arm brace on and held it out of the water. He agreed to let me drive but told me to be very careful.

I evaluated the potential challenges facing me. First was eating. I couldn't really cook with one arm, but I could drive to get take-out food or have it delivered or use the microwave. Meals for myself: one problem solved!

Next I had to figure out how to bathe, so I did a trial run in the bathroom with all my clothes on and Harley as my cheerleader. He always stood by the side of the tub when I was in it. Holding on with my good arm, I got into the tub and managed to get down on my knees. From that position I could bathe myself, and I knew I could get myself up with my one arm, so this problem was solved, too. I said, "Harley, I can do it! We can stay here. Thank God—we don't have to leave!" I can't explain how much it meant to me to be in my own home with Harley, except to say that my home was my safe haven and my refuge. I knew I could heal more quickly there than anywhere else. And I didn't want to lose my independence just because I had a broken arm.

I managed to drive myself the half mile to the office every day and work for a few hours. Even though I couldn't take my real estate clients out, I kept in touch with them by phone. I drove to the hairdresser to have my hair washed a few times a week so I could look presentable. I never missed a beat and I never skipped a day.

The day I had returned from Vermont, Michael had called to see how my trip was. I was dying to see him

again, but how was I going to do that when I couldn't
even comb my hair? Basically I was a physical wreck, and
I looked like one—sort of like Bart Simpson in a large
flannel shirt and pull-on pants. I gave him the news
about my arm and my disheveled, grossly modified
appearance, which didn't seem to faze him; after all, he
was a doctor.

Michael came to take me to dinner the next Saturday,
when my injury was about nine days old. I was able to
dress myself in slacks and my trusty flannel shirt with a
snap front that I was able to close with one hand, so that's
what I wore. My hair and makeup were drastically different
from our first meeting. It was snowing lightly, and Michael
put my coat on for me and helped me to the car. We went
to the Coach Grille for dinner. After the meal when I went
to the ladies' room, I had to ask Michael to help zip up my
slacks because I couldn't manage that myself. At home I
could lie on the floor and do it by myself.

During the next several weeks while my arm healed,
Michael took me to dinner, put my boots on, buttoned
up my coat, zipped up my pants when needed, and at
times carried my handbag—all done in an easy,
comforting, and humorous manner. On occasion he even
ran a comb through my hair. Sometimes people stared
at us when he helped me. I remember thinking to myself,
*This is one secure man who doesn't worry about how he
looks to others.*

During those months, the two of us learned a lot about who we were as individuals. We developed great respect for one another, shared a mutually dry sense of humor, and talked about our future goals. Becoming friends, we discovered how compatible we really were. I am now convinced that my mother looked down on me from the heavens and arranged for me to take that fall while I was skiing in order to slow me down and help me learn to be a little dependent on someone else. I had never let anyone take care of me before. I also think that if Holly could have handpicked a man for her Auntie Mal, Michael would have been the one. He is very smart, great looking, and a fabulous conversationalist.

My lengthy convalescence also gave me time to see Michael in his role as a loving father with his three children, as I was often there when he had telephone conversations with them. I had the opportunity as well to observe how attentive he was to his patients and how he made himself available for them. He was an exceedingly caring friend to me, not just in terms of thoughtfully helping me while my arm healed, but in listening and paying attention when I talked with him. I began to feel really comfortable talking things over together. This was a quality man, with no baggage other than a couple of other women he was dating casually at the time, since we hadn't yet decided to see each other exclusively. My friends nicknamed him "Dr. Delicious."

As Michael and I developed a deeper friendship, I learned more intimate details about him. Although he had not come from a family that abused alcohol, over the years, like myself, Michael became an alcoholic. He started drinking in high school, and in college he would occasionally binge drink. By the time he got to medical school, he was drinking regularly to quiet his mind at night. Upon graduation from medical school, drinking became a real problem for him. After some psychotherapy for himself for what he perceived as anxiety and depression, he decided to go into psychiatry to learn more about emotional illness. Years later, when he wanted to become sober, Michael had an epiphany, a spiritual awakening not unlike mine. As of the writing of this book, he has been sober, with the help of Alcoholics Anonymous and an assortment of other spiritual resources, for well over twenty years.

Because we share a similar history and a spiritual approach to our lives, Michael has been able to understand exactly where I have been on my path. We have a strong spiritual alignment in our careers as well as in our relationship. Realizing that not everyone has success in AA, he has spent his time since becoming sober developing and offering an alternative program for people dealing with alcohol dependence. His approach is personalized to each person, and, of course, he is able to keep the individual's situation completely confidential. It is a unique and very effective program.

Over dinner one night after we had been seeing each other for a few months, Michael and I talked about where we thought our relationship might be going. We discussed the possibility of an exclusive and intimate relationship. In sobriety, I had learned the importance of establishing a friendship before having sex, so we had spent these months really getting to know and like each other. We agreed we were great together and wanted to take our relationship to the next level. I told him I had flunked sharing my toys in the second grade and that he would have to do a little housecleaning of any other women in his life to make this work. Remember, I now had boundaries and knew clearly what I wanted. No secondhand crumbs for me—I was becoming an Alpha Chick! We agreed not to see anyone else.

When we made plans to see each other the next weekend, I suggested, "Why don't you bring a toothbrush?" The toothbrush was OK, but I made it clear I did not want him to move in! In time I was comfortable with his bringing more things over.

The next week, we planned our first romantic getaway to my family's home on Cape Cod. Of course, Harley was going, too. Michael arrived with his suitcase, which we put in the back of my SUV with Harley. When we arrived at the Cape, Michael's suitcase was slightly wet. He thought maybe it was a flipped water bowl, but

I knew differently: Harley was welcoming him into our family by marking his suitcase.

Dr. Delicious was so gracious about his peed-on clothes. This was a real test of his composure, his love for me, and his bemused tolerance of Harley. He knew only too well that Harley was my little man.

Michael and I were engaged to be married five months later and planned our wedding for June of 2003. He had a beautiful engagement ring made for me with the large stone from his mother's engagement ring along with two additional diamonds. My wedding band had all the diamonds from his mother's wedding band, reset in a new platinum band.

Our wedding was just perfect in every way, except for a little slipup with my wedding gown. Ten days before the wedding, a friend called to tell me she had read in the newspaper about a huge theft of wedding gowns from the bridal shop where I had bought my dress. When the shop owner wouldn't answer her phone, I got panicky and drove to her house. She told me my gown was one of the ones that had been stolen!

The dress had been ordered from New York, and it had already been altered to fit me. There was no way another one could be reordered and altered in time for the wedding. I started running around to bridal shops like a lunatic. A friend suggested I go to the Designer Bridal Outlet in Newton. I told the owner the story about my stolen gown and that my wedding was now in eight days, and she brought out an absolutely gorgeous *peau de soie* strapless Lazaro gown, with the most beautiful beading I had ever seen. It was exquisite and looked even more elegant when I tried it on. I even liked it better than the dress that had been stolen. However, it was a little too small and I was afraid it would not work out.

The shop owner said, "Don't worry," and walked me across the street to the most incredible seamstress with whom I have ever worked. The woman told me, "I'll take this apart and remake it, and it'll fit you like a glove." Then she promised me she would have all the alterations done in time for the wedding. I was thrilled! She made good on her promise and even made me a lovely tulle wrap for my shoulders, all piped with the *peau de soie* from the dress. When Michael came with me to pick up the gown, she took extra time to show him how to do up the buttons and arrange the wrap because he was going to help me dress for the wedding in our hotel suite. No worries about bad luck for us!

The day of the wedding, Michael gave me an incredibly beautiful pearl and diamond necklace with two lovebirds for a clasp. Of course I wore it that day. Our entire wedding day was like something right out of a dream. We were married in the Leslie Lindsay Memorial Chapel at the Arlington Street Church in Boston. We decided to walk each other in to the ceremony. Michael's three children read the Jewish wedding blessings in Hebrew and participated in the blended Catholic-and-Jewish ceremony. We held our reception for forty close friends and family just down the street at the beautiful Ritz Carlton Hotel. I felt like a fairy princess with my Prince Charming, and the reception looked like a dinner for royalty.

The day I married Michael was the greatest day of my life. The photographer took an amazing photo of the two of us walking down the street from the chapel to the hotel; we look as though we are floating. And not only did I get a wonderful husband, he came with three fabulous adult children with whom I have developed truly loving relationships.

My stepdaughter Ali is the oldest daughter. She is tall and beautiful and looks the most like Michael. She also has his easy temperament and his intelligence. Ali graduated from the Massachusetts Institute of Technology with a degree in mechanical engineering and then obtained a master's degree in mechanical engineering from Stanford. She is married to Raphael, and in 2009, our precious little granddaughter, Sophie, was born. The eldest child, my stepson Joseph, graduated with honors from the Tisch School of the Arts at New York University and studied at the Royal Academy of Dramatic Art in London. He is enormously talented, coaches actors and speakers in Los Angeles, and is married to an immensely artistic woman named Sabine. Lily, my younger stepdaughter, is also a very attractive young woman and was married to Bryan Harder in 2010. She graduated from Northwestern University and received her MBA from the ESADE Business School in Barcelona, Spain.

The Law of Attraction, which I talked about earlier, has surely been at work in my life. For a long time, I thought I would not have any children, even though I wanted them. Now I have three amazing children and an adorable granddaughter, too! When I shared with them that I was writing this book about my recovery from alcohol, they were very supportive and excited for me. Perhaps they will want to get involved with future Alpha Chick projects such as the website, blog, and multimedia ideas.

I hope my story will inspire you to find your own Dr. Delicious. Michael has encouraged me to write this book. He has been incredibly supportive, reading the manuscript and giving me useful feedback and ideas. He believes I have something important to share with other women and wants to see me do that. I guess he has seen firsthand how hard I have worked on my sobriety and personal growth. To have the man I love so dearly stand beside me on this journey makes it even more compelling for me. I had never really thought about getting married again. Yet when Michael proposed to me, I knew instantly that if I did not say yes I would make the greatest mistake of my life. To wake up every day next to someone who loves you, respects you, encourages you, and wants you to be the very best you can be is what I wish for every woman. We were created to live a life of joy and not suffering. The choice is ours to make.

Becoming an Alpha Chick and developing a new perception of my life prepared me for attracting the perfect partner. Once I was able to let go of my past, I could live fully in the present moment and set powerful intentions for my future. My relationships were no longer defined by past circumstances, but rather by what I was intending and wanting in my life. I had become very clear about what I wanted to attract through the five steps in the Alpha Chick Process, though I had not formally described them as such yet; the process did not get officially named until the spring of 2009. By my asking, believing, and then allowing, the ideal man was drawn into my life.

So I invite you to stop focusing on what you do *not* have. The energy and thought that you place on the existing lack creates more of the same. Instead, develop a detailed picture about the relationship that you would like to attract into your life. By practicing deliberate mental shifts, you can manifest marvelous things and bring that which you truly desire and deserve into your life.

Living Life as an Alpha Chick

Living my life as an Alpha Chick, I am aware now of my true potential and purpose. Self-awareness and serenity are my reality. Most of the time my life runs like a finely tuned piece of machinery, with all parts working in harmony with one another. I am no longer pulled in conflicting directions. I begin each day knowing and loving the woman I am. I appreciate everything I have: my husband, my health, my homes, and my work. And until March of 2010, I also had my precious Harley, who was such an important part of my morning ritual. He is now on the Rainbow Bridge waiting for me. Getting to this kind of clarity has been a process. It has taken time, patience, persistence, and lots of hard work. Since my epiphany, now so long ago, I can truly say that every year has been better than the last, and I know next year will be even better than this one.

What an exquisite journey it has been. I don't regret the past because it has led me to where I am today. I have been blessed to know several wonderful people along the way who have helped and inspired me. You, too, can start a personal transformation like this for yourself, with wonderful results! Once you make this commitment to yourself, you are taking your first steps to self-empowerment and improvement.

On December 31, 1988, the last day I touched alcohol, I made the commitment to change my life and become sober. In time, I discovered my spiritual essence—a connection with my higher power. I found a divine presence within me that was guiding me, and I never looked back. I was actively working in real estate and doing very well. I really loved it and would never have consciously done anything to jeopardize that. As my level of consciousness grew through sobriety, my path became more apparent and I discovered a deeper passion for my work. I shifted into high gear.

As I became aware of the powers of an Alpha Chick, I found myself propelled by a new commitment to be the very best realtor I could be and to learn as much as I could about my profession. I had thought many times of going back to college, but found instead that pursuing a more individualized program really worked the best for me. Even if your life takes some unorthodox turns and the traditional route doesn't work for you either, know that education is always available and attainable if you want it, and it is so very important.

I began attending classes, seminars, and workshops to pursue every designation that a realtor could obtain: Graduate Realtor Institute (GRI), Certified Residential Specialist (CRS), Leadership Training Graduate (LTG), and Accredited Buyer's Representative (ABR). This advanced training gave me greater knowledge and confidence in my ability to serve my clients, and my entire career focus changed. When I started out in real estate, I wanted to make money, and doing so was what it was all about for me. As an Alpha Chick, however, I no longer think about money the same way. I don't have to focus on it because I know that by being true to myself, money will flow into my life with ease. Instead, I think about the people who are my clients and how I can improve their lives. Helping others has been my motivation in real estate for years now, and I believe my clients know this.

One client, Joan, who later became the friend I introduced to you in my Acknowledgments, was going through a particularly difficult divorce. She had to sell the large house they had owned together. It had been on the market for months, and she couldn't afford to maintain it any longer. She needed to downsize and wanted to move into a condo. Joan was so stressed that other agents had been unable to work with her, and by the time she called me, she had fired two agents and been dropped by another.

I understood Joan's situation perfectly, having lived it myself, and I was able to treat her with empathy and kindness, while at the same time setting firm boundaries. I explained to her that she needed to step back and let me do my job. Because I was kind, honest, and firm, she trusted me and was willing to do what I asked. I was able to sell her house quickly and for more money than she had hoped for! Knowing Joan was worried about her finances, as she had been out of work for some time, I found a townhouse I thought she would like and told her about it, suggesting she go see it without me. She loved the place! I told her to make an offer directly to the owners and that I would not participate in the transaction so that a broker's commission would not increase the price of the property. She lived there for ten years and then bought another condo. I assisted her with that transaction, too.

Joan had been a loyal client since I sold her home, recommending me to everyone she could. I told her several times that if she got a real estate license, I could pay her for those referrals. Eventually she got her license as I had suggested. After telling me she wouldn't work anywhere else, Joan now works for my company and even helped me organize some of the material for this book.

As with Joan, I've been able to build strong, honest relationships with clients based on putting their interests first. These are relationships that have lasted for years, bringing me repeat business, referrals, and friendships.

I worked for Coldwell Banker from October of 1986 until February of 1990. In January of 1990, I met with Ed Davis, the owner of Dallamora Real Estate, the top-producing office at the time, who invited me to come to work for his company. I was very pleased with the offer and thought it was one I would eventually like to accept. However, I explained to him that I couldn't leave Coldwell Banker in the lurch because I was currently my office's top-producing sales agent and my leaving would really hurt my manager, whom I thought was my friend.

Several days after that meeting with Ed, I talked to my manager about the offer I'd received, assuring her that I would never do anything without discussing it with her first. She and I had shared some really personal details about our lives with one another—I about my drinking and she about her life issues. Because I believed we were friends, talking to her about my future career plans seemed like the right thing to do. I had numerous active listings at Coldwell Banker and thought I should sell those properties before moving on.

Two weeks later I left for a short vacation in Cancun, Mexico. You can imagine my surprise when, upon returning to the office, none of my colleagues even looked up from their desks to say hello as I came in. On top of my desk, I found a black plastic bag stuffed with the things that had been inside that piece of furniture. I asked the staff what was going on, and they said I had better talk to my manager, so I did. She told me that after the conversation we had before I went on vacation, she thought it best that Coldwell Banker and I part ways. Since I was thinking of leaving, she had decided it would be better to do it now. Furthermore, she had given all my listings and all my clients to other agents in the office. All of a sudden I had no job and no clients. Absolutely heartbroken that she had treated me that way, I quietly organized my things and left without another word.

I learned the hard way that although I believe honesty is the best policy, other people will not always respond to my honesty with the same kind of integrity I have toward them. However, because I had become an Alpha Chick, I was able to accept what had happened, forgive my manager, and move on to what turned out to be an even better opportunity. I no longer wasted my emotional energy on what I saw as a betrayal, because by then I knew that good was always in store for me.

I went right back to Ed Davis at Dallamora and told him exactly what had happened and that I was now available to join his team. He was happy to have me, and I worked very successfully at Dallamora until January 1, 1993. I was awarded their Top New Producing Agent and

Rookie of the Year awards, and was in their top tier of salespeople for as long as I worked there.

As an Alpha Chick, I view my colleagues in much the same way as I do my clients; I want to help them and share whatever I have learned that has made me successful. While at Dallamora, I taught the other agents two courses, one about listing presentations and the other about how to convert "For Sale by Owners" (FSBOs) into clients. As I gave out more of these "good vibes," they came back to me in strong relationships with my colleagues. Dallamora was a good place for me to work.

While I was there, a new company, ReMax, introduced an unusual concept in real estate agency management, in which agents pay for all their expenses but keep a larger percentage of the compensation. Under their system, agents ran their own businesses with their own profit-and-loss statements and paid all their own expenses, from rent to advertising and everything in between. I was certain this system would work for me— it resonated with my willingness to take complete responsibility for my work—and I decided it was time for me to make another move. It took some guts for me to do this at the time because I had just built my beautiful new home in Framingham, which meant increased expenses, and now I would be committing to assuming additional expenses associated with my work. But I did it and signed on with ReMax, leaving Dallamora on very good terms and grateful for the opportunity the company had given me. As a confident Alpha Chick, I was sure I would succeed. And I did!

I built my new ReMax business by hiring an office assistant to take care of the administrative work, which allowed me to increase the time I spent with clients. Then I hired a buyer's agent, who could provide specific help to our clients in their home searches. After three years, I became the top producer of the office—a Platinum Club member with multi-million-dollar sales figures. I was basically running my own small company at this point.

While at ReMax, I worked with a group of eleven other highly technically oriented agents from all over Massachusetts to develop and implement a specialized Web link that would allow clients to access the multiple listing service directly from an agent's website. We called this the Online Assistant. This was the first time ever that clients could go directly from a realtor's website to view multiple listings! Both ReMax and Century 21 bought the software, which was to revolutionize the real estate industry.

I had worked very well with another ReMax agent who was the company's former top producer, and he and I decided we could improve both of our businesses if we worked together in a partnership. So in 1995, we opened our own satellite office and grew our team to nine agents. One of the rewards of the Law of Attraction working in my life was that I found a wonderful space for our office only minutes from my home, which had been a specific goal of mine. My life was a lot more relaxed when I could be at the office and get home in nothing flat to have lunch with Harley.

Unfortunately, my partner would come in briefly in the morning and then disappear for the day. I ended up doing the lion's share of the work. I was starting to feel very uncomfortable with the arrangement I had made with him. I realized that I had to dissolve this partnership, as the situation had become completely untenable.

One night I was working at the office after ten o'clock when a contractor who knew me well saw my car as he drove by. He stopped and came in to make sure I was all right and found me sitting at my desk sobbing from exhaustion. I was preparing a purchase and sales agreement for a builder on a particularly complicated transaction. I had been working from sixty to eighty hours a week to make up for my partner's lack of attention to the business and to be sure our clients were well taken care of. I was overwhelmed.

My sobriety and newfound self-respect allowed me to inventory the situation and recognize that this partnership had become unhealthy for me. I could see there was now the potential for a disastrous outcome for my business. As an Alpha Chick, I was able to think clearly, evaluate my options, and move forward without fear or insecurity. I engaged the services of my friend Faith Easter, who is an attorney, and took the appropriate action to end the partnership, which was dissolved in 1998. Protected by self-love and sobriety, I had the ability to make the right choices and take good care of myself and my clients, whose interests were also at stake.

Again, because I practiced the five steps of the Alpha Chick Process, which you will learn about in detail in Part Two, I knew only better things were in store for me. They have helped me successfully manage unexpected turns in the road to always ensure a positive outcome for myself.

I continued to successfully operate a satellite office to the parent ReMax company for another two years. Because of this, I came to believe I could start my own real estate business and make that company a success. I also believed a company of my own would give me the best opportunity to help clients and the agents who worked with me. After planning throughout the fall, I formed my own corporation on December 1, 2000, and introduced MalDuane.com. I assumed the lease and all obligations of the office I had run for ReMax and changed the name over the door to mine! What an overwhelming sense of accomplishment, self-respect, and gratitude I felt the first time I looked at that sign. This was the result of thirteen years of hard work, mental focus, and attracting what I wanted.

When I began MalDuane.com, the Internet had just begun to change the structure of the real estate industry. While many companies much larger than mine would take a long time to understand what the Internet would mean to the real estate industry, I was on the leading edge of Internet marketing. I acquired several more designations—Senior Real Estate Specialist, e-Pro, and Real Estate Cyber Specialist—and utilized the wonderful new technology to expand my business very effectively. My office was the first independent real estate company in the greater Boston MetroWest area to have a website with access to a multiple listing service for clients, virtual tours, and e-mail marketing campaigns.

I was becoming recognized as an expert in the techniques of Internet marketing for real estate. My peers saw that my company's approach to this business was cutting edge. Instead of hoarding my knowledge to keep a corner on the marketplace, I was more than happy to share my business plan and systems with anyone who asked me. As an Alpha Chick, I had learned that a very important part of building my own strength and transformation was helping others and teaching them what I had learned, and I continue this practice to this day.

Eventually I was invited to travel all over the United States to share marketing and business-building concepts with other top producers. I did an interview for the

Certified Residential Specialist (CRS) national magazine and website. I also addressed Craig Forte's 3-Steps Marketing Group in Phoenix, which later offered me a retainer because I helped them market and sell a web-based product I was instrumental in developing. *Banker and Tradesman* magazine interviewed me and featured me on the cover a couple of times. As one of the top-producing realtors in the country, I was invited to Las Vegas by Floyd Wickman, one of America's preeminent real estate trainers, to participate in his Top Producer Panel, and I spoke before five hundred agents from all over the United States. I traveled to Phoenix again for a Mega Agent Marketing meeting, where successful agents nationwide were asked to create compelling direct-mail campaigns and toll-free advertising programs. I've also given numerous recorded interviews at no charge about how to build successful Internet marketing strategies, and my recordings have been distributed to realtors nationally. On two occasions, I've been a featured speaker at the Real Estate CyberSpace Society's annual convention, which has an attendance of more than thirty thousand agents.

I share my successes with you not to show you what a big shot I've become, but rather to illustrate how I have been able to develop my full power and potential by following the steps of the Alpha Chick process. I have grown so much, and with that growth has come recognition, personal fulfillment, and prosperity. My career has taken off like a rocket, but more important, I love what I am doing. Making more money has not been the primary objective in these pursuits; rather, it is a benefit that has come to me as a result of continually expanding my knowledge and my joy in helping others with what I have learned.

My real estate business has flourished and expanded every year. In 2003, my production was $50 million in sales! By the fall of 2004, I had made enough money to pay cash for an antique building in the historic district of Framingham, where my company, MetroWest Homes, is now located. I completely remodeled and restored the building, which is now one of the most recognized and admired structures in the area. I continue to make improvements to the building and rent offices to other professionals. This is an accomplishment in which I take great pride because it has helped the community as well as myself.

During the fall of 2006, when the market started to slow down, I was still doing a strong business, but not the huge numbers from previous years. The market further declined in 2007 and 2008 as the mortgage industry began to crumble. Like all realtors, I was affected by the horrific financial downturn that was having an impact on every industry in this country.

Regardless of the terrible economy and its disastrous consequences, however, I have not lost my optimism or my belief that we will recover. At

MetroWest Homes staff meetings and in one-on-one conversations, I continue to share my optimism and my own Alpha Chick Process with the agents who work with me. I've introduced them to a strong practice of positive and creative thinking. I encourage them to meditate and envision what they want to bring about in their lives, personally as well as professionally, and to believe in themselves and their own potential. I share all my many books and recordings from my Library of Love about the Law of Attraction and becoming successful. I like to believe these colleagues have been helped by my approach to life, learning valuable lessons they would never even have been exposed to in a typical real estate company. While many real estate companies and satellite offices have failed all across the country, the Alpha Chick approach to success, thoughtful analysis, and budget revisions has kept my company afloat, with doors open, doing business, and debt free.

Without my sobriety and positive mental shift, I would not have had the confidence in myself to take as many risks as I have in taking my business to higher levels. I experience an emotional and mental clarity that I did not have before. My faith in my business skills and the ability to shift my thoughts to more positive thinking when I become troubled have carried me through one of the worst financial declines in American history. I have analyzed the market and sought new areas for business. I work closely with my sales agents to help them believe in themselves and create innovative programs that bring in new clients. My primary goal has been to help my agents remain in business and stay afloat financially during this challenging economic situation, and I like to think my company has successfully turned the corner. I know the grace of God is with me.

My personal life has also experienced a huge transformation since I became sober. As described in "Dr. Delicious," in 2003 I married Michael, with whom I have a powerful and loving partnership. The ability to see and develop the person I truly am has led me down a path of self-respect, self-love, and fulfillment. The quality of the relationships I have developed with my family and my friends has become significantly better over the years. In the past, I always looked for approval from others. Now my self-worth comes from within, and I look for honesty and integrity first in my friends and colleagues. When you become completely honest with yourself, that honesty is reflected in all areas of your life. The kind of people I attract into my life has also changed. I've met so many inspirational human beings, including quite a few Alpha Chicks!

Every day I look around my beautiful home and thank God for all that I have. In 2006, I had a vision of owning a second home as a small getaway. I researched different areas in New England near the ocean that intrigued me and finally settled on Westport, Connecticut. I found out about some wonderful new construction that was to be built on the Saugatuck River and bought a small condo there. It is cozy, and we decorated it in fabulous warm hues of red, orange, and gold, accented by black furniture. From there, Michael and I can hop on the train and be in New York City in fifty minutes for shopping, dinner, or a play. When Michael's children or our friends visit us, they love our little getaway. We cherish the times we go to our shoebox on the Saugatuck for long weekends and holidays.

Since December of 1988, I have focused on building a strong body and staying healthy. I have worked over the years with several personal trainers, and since 2002, with an extraordinary woman named Rhonda Skloff. Rhonda first helped me when I was recovering from my broken arm, delicately working it back to full capacity. In 2008, she assisted me through two abdominal surgeries resulting from an appendectomy and postoperative complications. Because of her, I really have developed a disciplined exercise regimen, and I continue to work out daily. On days when I lack the motivation, she inspires me to do more.

Once I stopped drinking, eating healthy food became important to me, and I now pay a great deal of attention to nutrition. Several times when my discipline has flagged, I have gone to Weight Watchers. They have affordable programs that keep me accountable for what I am eating, and I count my points daily to stay on track. I support both my physical and emotional well-being with quality down time and a regular meditation practice. One day I bumped into a property manager who knew me from my ReMax days. He commented on how much calmer I seemed. He was actually very funny when he described my impatience from the 1990s. I am grateful that the changes I have undergone are apparent to others.

When I look at my life today, I see so many improvements in all areas. Practicing the five steps of the Alpha Chick Process has enhanced every aspect of my life—physical, mental, emotional, spiritual, and financial.

I am so blessed! I am happy, healthy, fulfilled, successful, and surrounded by love. I have everything I need and more. As a result, I want to share the knowledge of how to achieve these blessings with as many women as I can. The ability to tap in to this quality of life is within us all. We are all created equally; we just need to learn to access the divine presence within us. I feel confident that if you commit to and follow the steps outlined in Part Two of this book, you will learn, as I did, how to find the joy and success you are meant to have in your life.

Please Join Me!

I am thrilled that you have read the first part of *Alpha Chick*! It's likely you've experienced some identification with my personal story.

Perhaps it has triggered some soul searching about your own journey. I want to be able to connect personally with you to help to keep your momentum going.

If you would like me to communicate with you, my email is mal@alphachick.com.

You may also enjoy the FREE Class with Mal.

How to Stay on Track as an Alpha Chick

www.AlphaChick.com/freeclass

During this free class (which you can listen to immediately), you'll discover what to do from here to keep your momentum going. The journey of becoming ALL of who you were born to be as a magnificent, radiant, powerful, purposeful and prosperous Alpha Chick requires consistent intention and action. This class will give you specific steps to take from this point forward to experience the lasting success and fulfillment… and PEACE… you've been looking for!

It's easy! Just go to www.AlphaChick.com/freeclass to register for the FREE class, and you can listen right away.

Grandmother Duane wearing her diamonds

Grandmother Hickey with her mink stole

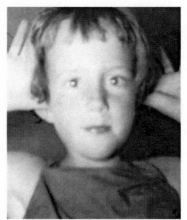

Mal with "picket fence" bangs

Mal with Oleg Cassini

Mal with Philip and Holly
at circus

Mal riding an elephant at the Barnum & Bailey Circus

My champion horse, Scooter

Holly and Mal in Paris

Dr. Delicious and Mal on their wedding day

Harley, Mal's Jack Russell Terrier

Children at the Katherine Holly School

PART TWO

The Five Steps

of the

Alpha Chick Process

Introduction:
Step Into Faith

Faith is a verb. It's our willingness to experience life as it unfolds in all of its pain and all of its promise.

—Joan Borysenko

In Part One, you read the story of my life, in which I explained all about the difficulties I faced and the mistakes I made. You saw how unhappy and desperate I became. You know that I identified the kind of woman I wanted to be as what I am calling an Alpha Chick, and that I found a way to become one, trading in my desperation for joy. By the last chapters in Part One, I had begun my life as an Alpha Chick.

Over the years, I began to understand that my journey of recovery consisted of a specific process. In Part Two, I share with you the practices that I developed and continue to follow every day. You will have the opportunity to do more than *read about* changing your life—you can become proactive about ensuring that positive and enduring changes happen.

The Alpha Chick process readily divides into five distinct stages, or steps, each of which includes its own unique actions. I'd like to share with you how they came about.

One particular morning during my daily meditation, the message was powerful and clear that faith in a power greater than myself, but which was also inherently within me and part of my nature, was the foundation of personal transformation. I realized that it was faith that had allowed me to go within and listen to the voice of the divine presence that freed me from self-imposed limitations.

This helped me to better understand what had happened during my personal epiphany on my last day of drinking. On that day, I knew death was close and sought God's help to save me. In that moment, I made a profound connection to the divine presence within myself and experienced a "soul knowing" of its existence, which I refer to as "faith." Suddenly I was no longer riddled by emotional pain, and I experienced an inexplicable knowledge that I had nothing to fear. When I surrendered in faith, God gave me the insight and the courage to see what I had to do to heal my life. When I let go of my ego and recognized the divine presence within, my new journey toward empowered wholeness began. The light of faith made my path visible to me.

So it is not surprising that the message I received that day in meditation went on to indicate that there are *five steps* and that their names spell out the word *faith*:

F   Focus
A   Acceptance and Attitude
I   Identification and Intention
T   Thoughts
H   Healing and Helping

Consistently following these faith-filled steps has changed my life dramatically and infused my existence with a joy and well-being that previously I would never have thought possible. I have been able to change the way I see my world and the way I live my life. Most important, my identity and my life are no longer defined by the experiences of my past. I refused to let my negative emotions control my life, and I gave up self-sabotaging habits such as alcohol and destructive relationships. These changes brought about a huge mental and emotional shift that gave me the freedom to live a life I had only dared to dream about instead of the life I thought I had no control over because of my negative choices and past experiences.

Faith is what both my mother and Holly, who exemplify for me so many qualities of an Alpha Chick, had so strongly, and which allowed them to persevere in the face of extremely challenging circumstances. It is the alpha and the omega, the beginning and the end, of where all the Alpha Chick steps lead. As always, from the beginning of the world, faith is a mystery. Like electricity, you can't explain it or see it but you can definitely feel its effects. You know when it is working.

Faith is both the process and the outcome. It directs and enables you to go within to find the power with which you were born. It shows you how to align yourself with God. With faith, you are able to see beyond the appearances of this world and connect with the underlying force for good in your life. In so doing, you become empowered to be the woman you were meant to be, an Alpha Chick living life at your full potential, surrounded by love, joy, and abundance.

Blessings to you on your journey!

Step 1:
Focus

"It is a process of diverting one's scattered forces into one powerful channel."

~ James Allen

The first step of the Alpha Chick Process is to go within yourself and find the power with which you were born. It stresses the importance of a regular connection with your higher power:

I focus my consciousness daily on the divine presence within through a spiritual practice.

Women come into this world with extraordinary power, energy, and intuitive knowledge, but we are rarely taught how to access and develop these gifts. As small children we are frequently told to behave, be quiet, and be "good little girls." We grow up with this "good little girl" mentality, putting aside our true identities, and our souls languish in the process. By tapping in to the divine presence within us, we access a renewed will and desire to move forward once again.

For the twenty-four years during which I drank alcohol, I was on a different frequency from the rest of the world. By this I mean that my emotions and my reactions to life circumstances were clouded and distorted by alcohol. I saw life "through a glass, darkly."[1] My perceptions of reality were skewed, and I couldn't think clearly. I developed a repetitive pattern of self-destructive behaviors, particularly in relationships with men. In a word, I was miserable.

After drinking obsessively for many years, I hit bottom at the very end of 1988. I had not been ready to do anything to help myself until my life became so unbearable that I was incapacitated and I wished that I would die. I stayed in bed for a couple of days, under the covers. Dressed in my favorite leopard PJs and curled up in a fetal position, I longed to return to my mother's womb. My body was gripped with fear. I was hiding from the negative emotional patterns that had run my life for so many years—God forbid they would jump out of the closet and drag me by my hair down the stairs to get another drink. I knew I could not go on this way. My life was like a piece of fabric woven from destructive relationships, self-sabotage, and damaging choices. I had reached my lowest point and begged God to hear my prayers.

Every person has her or his own pain tolerance level. The first portion of this book describes in detail the huge amount of emotional pain I had to go through before I was willing to admit defeat and ask for help. When the consequences of my drinking finally threatened my life, I was desperate enough to go to an Alcoholics Anonymous meeting. There it was suggested that I get down on my knees and ask my higher power to show me the way to live my life without alcohol.

The first three steps of AA's twelve-step program, as cited in the *Alcoholics Anonymous Big Book*, are:

1. We admitted we were powerless over alcohol—that our lives had become unmanageable.
2. We came to believe that a Power greater than ourselves could restore us to sanity.
3. We made a decision to turn our will and our lives over to the care of God *as we understood Him*.[2]

After my first AA meeting, I realized that I had taken Steps One, Two, and Three. I had admitted my failure and powerlessness, and I had asked God to help me. I had been introduced to a group of like-minded individuals who were willing to help me with more compassion than

I can describe or repay. These wise and empathic people had years of experience dealing with issues similar to mine. I was able to converse and share without embarrassment with others who had from two to more than twenty years of sobriety. Finally, I felt like I belonged somewhere. When I first arrived in the halls where the AA meetings were held, the realization that I was not alone with my problem lifted my spirit. The feeling I had at these meetings reminded me of how I'd felt when I walked around with my "blanky" as a very small child; I'd felt secure wrapped in that tattered, pink-and-white, threadbare blanket.

If you happen to be an alcoholic, Alcoholics Anonymous is a caring and multidimensional support group that can help you start your journey of self-discovery and begin to build your life toward where it is meant to be. Their twelve-step program has been utilized around the world to help people in recovery. It definitely pointed me in the right direction toward becoming a healthy and empowered individual. Other programs built upon the twelve steps of AA are now available to help people deal with a variety of substance abuse and addiction problems. When making such monumental changes in your life, finding a support group is highly recommended. It not only establishes a level of accountability for what you are trying to do, but also gives you a needed support system during challenging times in the process.

Today, with the assistance of the Internet, you can use Google or other search engines to find hundreds of resources to get help for any type of addiction. There are many options for outpatient treatment programs, blogs, forums, twelve-step programs, and chat rooms where you can maintain confidentiality while getting help with your particular problem. If your addiction has progressed beyond that possibility, you need to consider getting medical help in an inpatient detoxification facility or from a physician who specializes in such conditions. As women, we sometimes are embarrassed to admit our dependencies. It takes a very strong woman to openly acknowledge her weaknesses. But remember that your problem can only begin to be solved when you admit that you have a problem.

With the assistance of a few friends and my sponsor, for ninety days I went to AA meetings daily and then twice a week after that for my first year. I followed every suggestion that was made: attend meetings daily, read the *Big Book* of Alcoholics Anonymous, don't date, and follow the twelve steps. I read everything I could get my hands on about becoming a sober woman. I was on my way to never picking up another drink. It was time to look at Step Three again and surrender to a power greater than myself; I was ready to silence my mind and begin the journey of self-discovery.

For me, the first step to becoming an Alpha Chick was to pray, meditate, and open myself to the divine presence in a very specific, focused way. Every morning between 6:00 and 7:30, I would read new affirmations that I had written and then I would meditate for a few minutes, increasing the time as my practice became stronger. Consistency brought me comfort and the connection to a new source of energy. My mind became calm and my intention was to align with my higher power.

After doing this for several weeks, one day I received the gift of understanding and came to believe I could be restored to sanity. This illumination came to me like the proverbial lightning bolt. I had finished meditating and was on my knees praying when this overwhelming feeling of peace and love came over me. For the first time since early childhood, I felt safe and also free. Suddenly I was in touch with a power, a divine presence, that I had not known was within me. This power was greater than my alcoholism and greater than my past failures. I became willing to do whatever it would take to change my life, and I now believed my life could change. I was no longer plagued by the sharp pain of my mistakes, and I felt the divine presence inside of me was helping me to forgive myself for all my previous errors in judgment. I felt truly loved and cherished for perhaps the first time in my life.

This new knowing of the presence of the divine in my life had been ignited by the scorching flame of pain.

Though I had continued to do it, drinking had stopped being fun a long time before, and I was suffering from depression and self-destruction. Getting in touch with the new light in my soul enabled me to make changes. There wasn't an ounce of resistance left in me. My new connection with God told me I could live without drinking, and with concentrated attention I committed to overcoming it. This was the beginning of the wonderful journey that is now my life.

I deeply yearned to be a different woman. I wanted to feel that I had power and control over myself. I wanted well-being and to know that my life had purpose. The term Alpha Chick had not come to me yet, but I knew I wanted the things it represents. I began to understand that I was responsible for my own happiness—that life situations happened, but they did not *create* my happiness or my sorrow. In partnership with the divine presence within me, I discovered I had the strength to change—I had the choice to stay in this dreadfully depressed state, feel sorry for myself, and live as a victim of my circumstances—or I could change my thoughts.

But what were my thoughts?, I wondered. Crammed into my mind were thousands of ideas, many of them from the negative patterns and beliefs from the "Old Mal." How could I sort through all of this?

As I continued to meditate and focus on this new connection with God, my ego voice, that endless chatter in my head, began to subside, and I felt a new strength, a power previously unknown to me. By ego I mean my external self, that part of me that was self-serving and critical, controlling my behavior by its identification with external reality and values. When that part of me receded, I surrendered myself to my higher power, and I was able to look inward for my true identity and purpose. I began to hear a different voice in my head, and a warm, soothing sensation of comfort gradually came over me. My mind became clear. My goals were: (1) not to drink and (2) to turn my life around. By not drinking, I could stay tuned in to that inner strength and knowing. I had thought about not drinking before but never with the same conviction.

You may wonder how the first step to becoming an Alpha Chick is different from the first three steps of Alcoholics Anonymous. The first step of the Alpha Chick Process is about connecting to the divine presence within you with which you were born, then making a commitment to connect daily with that presence and its guidance. It is about focusing on your life so you see it more clearly, then bringing it into alignment with your aspirations. You engage in a deep inner concentration that brings forth your most painful thoughts. Once you clarify the problem, you can pursue the remedy. This practice is not necessarily tied to having been an alcoholic.

You don't have to have overcome alcoholism to become an Alpha Chick, but you do need to be free from addictions, because they distort your thinking and prevent you from achieving the things you want in life. I am thrilled to share with you that my last drink was, as I've mentioned, the last day of December in 1988. Now I never think of alcohol and it is not a factor in my life. If you are dealing with a substance or behavioral addiction, your homework starts here. It is impossible to think with a rational mind or connect to the frequency most of the world is on when you are under the influence of an addiction, whether it is to alcohol, drugs, food, gambling, sex, rage, or anything else you may be hooked on.

If you are one of the lucky ones who do not have an addiction to overcome before becoming an Alpha Chick, you can immediately begin working on establishing your own connection with your higher power and learning how it will work for you. How do you do that? I wish I could give you a simple formula or an easy answer, but because we are such unique creatures, each of us must find our own way. The key thing to remember is that regardless of what has happened in your life, you are a spiritual being, a child of the infinite universe, a child of the light. The universe and its creator wish you well. You were created to experience joy and fulfillment.

If you want to become an Alpha Chick, you will need to find the path that's right for your personal relationship with the divine presence within, your source of strength, hope, and empowerment. You may choose to do this in a religious setting—in a church, synagogue, or any other holy sanctuary, even one of your own making at home— or in the woods, by the ocean, or in your bedroom or your backyard. Regardless of how you access this loving, creative presence, know that once you do, it will be with you always, wherever you go and whatever you do.

I have continued my own daily spiritual practice since that first day in 1989. Although I was raised a Roman Catholic, I don't need to be in a church to experience the divine presence. I renew my connection every day in my home or wherever I find myself when I am traveling away from home. I find that becoming very quiet, unplugging from my outer world, and focusing on my inner being and the energy I feel in my body enables me to open to and align with the inherent joy, wisdom, peace, consciousness, creativity, abundance, and power of God. I have created a special space in my home for meditation, with a comfortable chair, a scented candle, and pictures of the people and things I love. I sit there quietly and commit myself to the divine presence and to receiving whatever messages it has for me that day.

Meditation is a spiritual practice. Spiritual writer and speaker Jiddu Krishnamurti, in his teachings about God delivered in a lecture in 1949, said, "Meditation is a process of understanding oneself. And when one begins to understand oneself, not only the conscious but all the hidden parts of oneself as well, then there comes tranquility. When the upper mind is tranquil, then the unconscious, the hidden layers project themselves."[3] I have noticed over time that the quality of my life is a reflection of the *consistency* of my daily spiritual practice. The more focused and disciplined I am, the greater joy and balance I experience. The guidance I have received in meditation has led me to make sound choices and empowering changes in my life.

I realized through the first step of the Alpha Chick Process that I was no longer going to consider myself a victim. In *Practicing the Power of Now*, bestselling author and mystic Eckhart Tolle says, "A victim identity is the belief that the past is more powerful than the present, which is the opposite of the truth."[4] I recognized how I had carried old heartaches and sorrows in my mind for years, projecting the feelings from my past into my present situation. My suffering was caused by an attachment to my past. My fears began when I was a small child and carried through all my adult relationships until I stopped drinking. Once I was prepared to let go of my past, I could also let go of my fears and, consequently, my suffering.

Eugene Holden, practitioner coordinator for the World Ministry of Prayer of the nondenominational United Centers for Spiritual Living, states in the August

2009 issue of *Science of Mind* magazine: "Nonattachment is the ability to let go of the misperceptions. It is the ability to let go of the pain from the past. Nonattachment is accepting what is."[5] I was trading my negative attachment to the past for knowledge of my true identity, which was the opposite of all the fears I had felt for so long. Your inner guidance shows you how to let go of your painful past so you can engage fully in the present.

As I surrendered to the divine within, I was able to release past experiences that no longer served me. Through this focused practice of spiritual connection, you, too, will begin to see yourself and the possibilities for your life in an entirely new way. You will become empowered. You will begin the miraculous process of changing yourself, and this will give your life a divine inspiration you might never have imagined! It will help you to free yourself from the prison of the past events of your life, no matter how terrible they may have been.

My desire is to help you discover the divine presence that is inside you. I believe that my journey is part of a bigger picture and that I have been inspired to share my story in order to show you that you have the ability to overcome adversity in your life just like I have.

Perhaps everything I've said about finding your connection to the divine presence within you sounds like hokum and mumbo jumbo to you. You may be thinking to yourself, *What is she talking about? I can't do that!* But if what you've been doing in your life so far hasn't worked, I ask you now to give this a try. Take some quiet time and ask for a connection to the divine presence within yourself, then wait and see what happens. I think you will be wonderfully surprised. As Jesus said in Matthew 7:7, "Ask and you shall receive. Seek and you shall find. Knock and the door will be opened."[6]

Focusing on and committing to a specific relationship with the divine presence is the foundation of the five steps for living the life of an Alpha Chick. It is the foundation on which you will build your new life and on which your alignment will continue to grow. You don't have to consciously recognize this bond all the time, but it will always be there. Take time and be gentle with yourself until you feel you have reached this energy within the soul of your being. This is a process that takes time, patience, compassion toward yourself, and self-love. Over time, your connection to the divine presence within you will strengthen. You will recognize when it deepens; a sense of well-being will soothe you, comfort you, and uplift you to move forward with your life.

Action Guide Exercise: Step #1

1 Print out the Alpha Chick Action Guide.

2 Read the suggestions on starting a meditation practice. (Page 2)

3 Answer the questions about your experience on Page 3.

If you don't have your guide yet,
please go to:
www. AlphaChick.com/actionguide

Step 2:
Acceptance and Attitude

"Acceptance of what has happened is the first step to overcoming the consequences of any misfortune."

~ William James

Now that you have begun to work on finding your connection to the divine presence within you, what comes next to bring you fulfillment and joy? Step 2 of the Alpha Chick process is:

I accept disappointments, fear, and sorrows so I may free myself from a past that no longer serves me, and I consciously change my attitude so that I may live the joyous life that is always available to me.

For someone who had struggled as long as I had, *accepting* the circumstances of my life was an enormous step. It was December 31, 1988, and

I could physically feel the toll my drinking and misery were taking on me. Most visibly, it was evident in my face. The face that had been on billboards and in magazines and TV commercials looked much older than its years. I felt sad when I looked in the mirror—my eyes were dark and lifeless, and my face showed signs of puffiness. Finally I was ready to admit to myself and others that my addiction to alcohol had caused my *misery*. I accepted that I was an alcoholic and I accepted responsibility for my drinking. Never before had I done that. My ego had always told me I was in control. If you had ever suggested to me that I had a drinking problem, I would have been tempted to poke your eye out with the toothpick from my martini olive!

Accepting my alcoholism allowed me to make the commitment to practice the program I needed to recover from my addiction. I had lost all my fight, resistance, and need to control. All that was left was a physically ill, emotionally challenged woman who wanted to make things right, who wanted to change her life. The connection to the divine presence within that I had acquired through Step 1 of the Alpha Chick process gave me the willingness and strength to change.

Here is an overview of some of the things I did, and still do, to work Step 2 in my life. I recommend you try them, too:

• Say the "Serenity Prayer" (used in AA) often.

• Make a deliberate, conscious choice to think and be positive.

• Use specific tools to help replace old negative thoughts and reactions with specific, new, positive ones. Things that work for me include writing down problems, then throwing away the paper on which they're written; putting my desires in an Attraction Box; keeping a Gratitude Journal and annual Gratitude Lists; and reciting the Alphabet of Gratitude. (More about these tools follows.)

• Develop the understanding that you really can change the way you respond to events by changing your attitude.

First, the "Serenity Prayer" became my guide:

God, grant me the serenity to accept *the things I cannot change [people, places, and things], courage to change the things I can [my attitudes], and the wisdom to know the difference.*[1]

I began my day reciting this little prayer and it was the last thing I said at night. It helped me to accept responsibility for all the mistakes I had made. I acknowledged all the poor choices in my life, all the failed relationships, and the fact that I drank too much, and I fully recognized it was time for a change. Before sobriety, I had blamed other people for my unhappiness and fought against what had happened to me. For years, I carried my entire past with me, hanging on to every painful moment, thought, and heartache. I had lived life as a victim of all my unsuccessful relationships for more than twenty-five years. The emotional energy required to do that was exhausting. How much easier my days became when I gave up resisting the truth.

Acceptance came when I was able to say to myself, "OK, I made mistakes—these things happened. But that was then, this is now. How am I going to make myself feel better *now*?" When I accepted responsibility for what had occurred in my life, I was able to let go of blaming other people for my unhappiness. I understood that I, and no one else, was responsible for my happiness. When I realized this, I began to understand as well that with this responsibility came the power to change my life. I didn't have to wait for someone else to make me happy—I could make myself happy. I didn't have to live as a victim anymore! Finally, I "got" what my mother had tried to tell me so many times when she'd said, "Get over it." She wasn't being insensitive; rather, what she had meant was to accept whatever had happened that I was unhappy about and then let it go—put it behind me and get on with my life.

As part of taking responsibility for my own happiness, I began to make an intense effort to keep myself in the present moment. I slowly learned to develop what I call *neutrality* to the situations around me. I intentionally changed my *attitude* toward things that bothered me and shifted my focus to think about what I desired. If someone or some event infuriated or depressed me, I now adopted an observing awareness rather than being judgmental. I was able to look at outcomes and potentials instead of just reacting emotionally to life events. For example, I no longer judged my relationship with Paul, the young lawyer. I actually developed an attitude of gratitude—if I had not known Paul, I might not have become sober. What was once a disastrous situation actually brought me to my path of recovery.

You could call this new perspective "living in the comfort of the gray zone of awareness and consciousness." Nothing was black and white anymore. I refused to label things as good or bad. In the past, my life had consisted of highs and lows. I was either exhilarated or down in the depths of sadness. I gave up the peaks and valleys in exchange for balance. When I practiced neutrality, I would awaken with peace of mind. I became more centered, rounded, and flexible. I suggest that you begin and end your day by saying the "Serenity Prayer" and observe the changes it brings in your life.

As I continued to work on acceptance of my life's disappointments, I became aware of a gradual shift in my attitude. I was becoming more positive! I bought every book I could find about how to acquire and maintain a positive mental attitude, such as those by Napoleon Hill, Emmet Fox, James Allen, Clement Stone, and Anthony Robbins. All of these inspirational thinkers explained the importance of exercising mental and emotional control for a truly successful life, and they all gave suggestions about ways to do that. I would encourage you to read as much as you can about positive thinking. Norman Vincent Peale's *The Power of Positive Thinking* might be a good place to start in learning about how a change in your attitude will change your life.

I gradually came to understand that I had control over my attitude. I had never realized this during all the years I was so miserable. This was huge for me. It took time and a great deal of practice and vigilance to develop a consistent positive mental attitude in my personal life. For whatever reason, I had always maintained this attitude in business, but my personal life was different— I really had to work at this piece of my transformation.

Here's an example of how my changed attitude affected the outcome of a potentially volatile situation. In 1992, my ex-husband, Ken, called to say that he was going to be in Framingham for a day and wanted to get together. I had not seen him in the six years since our divorce, and the thought of a face-to-face meeting with him made me very anxious. I kept thinking about how he would probably be drunk and attack me verbally as he had in the past. Then I decided to shift my attitude about the meeting and imagined a freeing and healing experience for me. I held this thought in my mind, picturing myself happy, and silently repeated, *My life is complete and I am liberated from past feelings*, right up until I arrived at the agreed-upon meeting place.

As I walked into the restaurant, Ken jumped off his chair and welcomed me with a radiant smile! Our conversation that afternoon was easy and pleasant. In fact, he talked at length about how much he missed me. Ken was still drinking, and he was definitely affected by the fact that I was not. I shared with him my realization that I was an alcoholic, and I made amends for any pain I might have caused him. Making amends, which is step nine of AA's twelve-step program, is very critical to the healing process. It was one of the nicest conversations I ever had with him. I was able to look at him with compassion, and I felt no resentment or anger from the past. I walked away from our meeting with an entirely new perspective on the failure of our relationship and marriage, realizing that I had contributed as well as he to their demise.

Two years later, Ken was stricken with cancer and called to tell me how sick he was. I felt genuine compassion and assured him that he would be in my prayers. He died about eighteen months later. I am so grateful that my attitude shift allowed me to let go of all my previous bad feelings so that I could send caring and loving thoughts to the dying man whom I had experienced as tormenting me so severely years before. I know Ken saw that my caring and concern were real. He was an alcoholic just as I had been, but one who never became free from the power of alcohol over him or achieved sobriety.

Today I am constantly asked, "How are you so positive all the time?" I explain the huge amount of work I had to do to make this shift in the way I look at life, and that I am working on accessing my full potential. What this means is that when I am in daily contact with the divine presence, the guidance within me, I am more able to live from that place of joy, love, creativity, and peace inherent within me. I found that with acceptance and an attitude shift I could open my world to many more options and usually a better outcome to daily situations. You are born with the ability to do the very same thing. The good news is that you can take control of your life and move beyond victimization. Maya Angelou said it so well: *"If you don't like something, change it. If you can't change it, change your attitude. Don't complain."*[2]

I think we all know that there are things that happen that we cannot change, no matter how hard we try. This includes the actions of other people and how they live their lives, as well as the many events outside of our control. For example, I had wanted to change the outcome of my relationship with Tony. I was obsessed with thoughts of what I could have done so that he wouldn't have broken up with me. I kept thinking, *What is wrong with me that he ended the relationship?* I played it over and over in my head. As women, many of us have been taught to assume full responsibility for the outcome of *any* situation we are in; all the "what-ifs" and "should haves" are the ways we blame ourselves for things we cannot change.

The truth was that there was nothing I could have done to change the outcome of that situation. However, I could have changed how I *felt* about the breakup, except I didn't know that at the time. Had I the tools to do this, I could have avoided a lot of unhappiness. On the other hand, I believe we are here to learn, and that some of our lessons may be more painful than others. The really difficult lessons that come in the form of catastrophic life experiences sometimes help you become more open to finding the voice and the power of the divine presence within. Then you can be directed toward the transformation of your life.

How simple it sounds: "Change your attitude." But it took much work and absolute honesty with myself. One by one, I played all the old reruns in my head and slowly developed a new attitude for each one. I made a list of those disappointments with which I had the most difficulty and then wrote them individually on small sticky notes, using the following format. You can write whatever words you are comfortable with so they will work best for you.

> Today *[insert date]* I release the *[insert whatever you feel: anger, fear, resentment, etc.]* I feel against *[insert name of the person]* for *[insert what happened that led you to feel the way you do, such as "hurting my feelings"]*. I also release my fear of *[insert whatever you want to let go of, such as "rejection that creates a terrible knot in my stomach"]*.

By writing down the particular anger, fear, resentment, or sadness I felt, I was more able to own and accept it. Next, I tore or crumpled up the paper and burned it or threw it away. If it happened to be something really awful, I tore it into small pieces and flushed it down the toilet. (Thankfully, this never had a bad effect on the plumbing in my house, but I can't guarantee that for you!) Then I crossed the matter off my original list and internally released it to my higher power to manage. I was no longer responsible for the problem or its solution and was free to go on with my life. Over the years, I have found this symbolic step of identifying and throwing a problem away incredibly liberating. It is a simple action that is wonderfully empowering. I made a ritual out of this practice and still do it today.

There is a Buddhist belief that all beings are given ten thousand joys and ten thousand sorrows. We will all have many feelings that arise with which we will have to cope; bad things and sad things happen to everyone. However, the power within you that you access through your focused connection to your higher power helps you accept life's events and develop the attitudes that serve you. When I stop listening to my ego voice and concentrate on the divine presence within, I find my personal power. If not, the ego restrains my willingness to change—its perspective is always very judgmental and one-sided, and it pulls me from my true self and divine path. The mean-spirited, degrading little "mini-me" voice is constantly trying to throw me under the bus and keep me handcuffed to my past. However, I am pleased to report that because of my diligent work with the Alpha Chick Process, my current relationships are no longer a reflection of my painful past experiences. I trust that through building on Step 1 as a foundation, and practicing Step 2, you will have the capacity to find a safe path through your life's challenges, just as I have.

Be assured that I am not perfect. My life continues to have ups and downs, and there are still times when I am gripped by anger, fear, or resentment. But now I know just what to do. I put the problem on a sticky note and trash it.

I also deal with things that upset my daily balance by meditating and intentionally reframing the way I think about them. As an example, in 2009, a situation occurred that filled me with fear. I received the town's bill for real estate taxes on the building I own that houses my real estate company. The taxes, already substantial, had increased by a whopping 30 percent, and had doubled in only four years! I was so upset I almost hyperventilated. I went into panic mode, thinking, *How am I going to pay this bill? Where am I going to get the money? I'll have to apply for an abatement. What if I don't get it? The economy is too bad to raise the rent. If I do, the tenants will leave!* and on and on—I was really scared. Real estate sales were way off due to the problems with the economy, and the company's revenues had dropped. Before I got the tax bill, I had been proud that I had been able to keep the company strong and solvent, and that my sales agents were working, but now I wasn't so sure. I was a wreck for four or five days. I started running around putting together an appeal for an abatement, which I was sure the town wouldn't grant.

Thankfully, I calmed down enough to realize that I needed to bring this problem into my daily meditation. When I quieted my mind, I asked for guidance from the divine presence within me. During my meditation, I received a clear message that told me, "You have always managed before, and this time will be no different. You will find a way to pay this bill just like you have paid all your other bills. Don't worry." Then I experienced a profound shift from anxiety and worry to a release of tension as I changed my attitude about the whole situation. I saw the tax bill as a problem I could solve, looked for ways I could adjust my expenses, and found some. Money became available, and I paid the bill.

My goal is to do more than just free myself from the negatives—I want to attract good into my life. By using what I have learned about positive thinking and visualization, I have improved and expanded the acceptance-and-release process with the addition of a fancy red leather box I call my Attraction Box. In it, I put all my requests for what I want to attract into my life for my higher power to manage.

By now, I have a wonderful collection of little notes in my Attraction Box, and I go through them all every year on New Year's Eve. Any requests still in the manifestation process stay in the box, while all the ones that have been fulfilled go on my Gratitude List for the year. There is no better way to start a new year than with being grateful; it creates such a positive flow of abundant energy. To give you a model, here are my Gratitude Lists for 2007 and 2008:

Gratitude List 2007

Clean mammogram

New clients John and Tara

Harley is doing really well.

New friend Dorothy

Weekend getaways

Michael Russer Internet marketing boot camp

Holly's school in West Africa

European vacation

Ann's friendship

Surviving a tough real estate market

Meeting Elton John at "We Are Family"

Working out with Rhonda

Youthful, energetic appearance

Gratitude List 2008

Harley made another miraculous recovery.

Michael's continued support and patience

Good recovery from appendicitis

Two beautiful homes that I love

Consistency in spiritual practice

New mortgage at 4.85 percent

Alpha Chick's progress

Cruise with the kids

All my family has good health.

Kept business going

Michael's kids are all doing really well.

I do more than compile a yearly Gratitude List, however. I also make daily entries in my Gratitude Journal. At the end of the day, I reflect on the good things that have happened and write them down. The entries don't necessarily have to be about major events. Sometimes things like just having a nice chicken salad sandwich for lunch or that Harley, though aging, was behaving like a happy puppy have been enough to help me keep a positive focus on the day.

Another helpful practice is reciting the Alphabet of Gratitude. You can do this anywhere and anytime—while you're sitting in traffic or in your dentist's waiting room, or trying to combat insomnia. Begin with the letter A and think of something you are grateful for that begins with that letter—for example, *apples*—so wonderful in the fall. Continue as far in the alphabet as time permits, such as my comfortable *bed*, my *car* started today, etc. These tools are terrific attitude builders.

The process of releasing negative events and constructing a positive attitude without attachment to an outcome has truly changed my life. The most powerful example of an attitude of acceptance that I have seen personally was that of my niece, Holly. I am reminded of her enormous ability to accept things the way they were. From an early age she came to terms with her diagnosis of hemophilia, and she lived gracefully and with an exceptionally positive attitude. When her health problems became more complicated, she accepted her situation with dignity and displayed amazing courage and great inner strength. I think Holly was able to remain strong because she didn't waste any of her precious energy on anger about her illness or in misery and self-pity over her fate; rather, she wanted to comfort the family and alleviate *our* fears! Holly was able to do this because she was prepared in her mind for the course ahead of her, which would, of course, include her death, while the rest of us were never fully accepting of, and thus were not prepared for, this inevitable outcome. Her doctor marveled at Holly's strength and determination to manage all the medications she was required to take daily. I believe Holly's acceptance and her incredible attitude extended her life longer than her several prognoses had predicted.

I hope the previous suggestions about ways to accept the things you cannot change while changing your outlook on life will be helpful to you. You may find other ways to practice Step 2, and I encourage you to share them with me and the greater Alpha Chick community at AlphaChick.com.

When you change your attitude, you will change the quality of your life. You have the ability to create what you can envision for yourself. The changes I made in my life were not predicated on money or material desires, but on a clear purpose and a burning desire to change my past destructive patterns. I am filled daily with gratitude for the blessed life I now live. I have learned firsthand the power of acceptance and the value of a positive mental attitude. Today, while there may be things I still aspire to, there is nothing I lack. Recently, I was trying to think of anyone with whom I would trade places and couldn't think of another set of circumstances or body I would rather be in.

My most sincere wish is for you to live your life with happiness and abundance. Having read this far, you are on your way to reaping life's rewards as an Alpha Chick. Step 3 will help you continue on your glorious journey!

Action Guide Exercise: Step #2

1 What is the first thing you need to stop resisting and accept as is? (Page 4)

2 Take a deep breath and exhale repeating three times what you are accepting. (Page 4)

3 What is your most nagging negative attitude? (Page 4)

4 Prepare a gratitude list for the past six months. (Page 5)

If you don't have your guide yet,
please go to:
www. AlphaChick.com/actionguide

Step 3:
Identification and Intention

*"We can't solve problems by using the
same kind of thinking we used when we
created them."*

~ Albert Einstein

Accepting that my life wasn't working and
developing a positive attitude was a powerful
second step, but then what? My life had felt
like a tornado's funnel and I was in the middle
of it with all the debris that had been swept
up along the way. Though I was moving in a
healthier direction, I was still overwhelmed by
what was not working in my life.

It was time to move into what I later
codified as Step 3 of the Alpha Chick Process:

*I identify negative behaviors that block
my potential and set intentions for
positive actions.*

With this goal in mind, the next action I took to clean the debris out of my life was to review the areas that were in turmoil and write out a list of everything I was doing that caused me pain or wasn't working for me. I knew I must do this honestly and completely. I spent a whole day itemizing all the things I did that ended up hurting me and sabotaging the quality of my life. At first, I felt completely overwhelmed by recognizing so many aspects of my behavior that weren't serving me. But I continued to work on the list and started to see that everything fell into one of four categories: mental/ emotional, spiritual, physical, and financial/career. This may be the most difficult step to complete. It requires complete and truthful self-analysis.

For me, my mental/emotional list far outweighed the other categories. I also saw that the items on the mental/emotional list had an impact on the items in all the other categories. How could I pull these various pieces together instead of having a thousand different ones, looking like a refrigerator door covered with annoying little magnets? The idea came to me to design what I now call the Alpha Chick Attraction Quadrant Sheet, on which I neatly organized my four groups. (My Attraction Quadrant Sheet is provided at the end of this chapter.)

To give a context for this, I want to refer back to the cake analogy I used in Part One. Describing it once to Michael, I told him my life was like a cake and that I was creating the recipe with all the ingredients I wanted to put in. He thought it was very appropriate. When our relationship became serious, I realized he could be the *frosting* on my cake. I think that describes perfectly how our partners should fit into our lives. I must admit that I had been one of those women who thought that a partner, in my case a man, was the *cake* and that the right person would make my life complete. Many women make the mistake of making their partner the foundation of their happiness and personal success, when that person should complement our lives rather than being the source of our personal identities. And actually, *healthy* people prefer mates who are independent and don't cling to them for the completion of themselves.

What I came to understand is that we are each responsible for our own cake—we choose our own ingredients and we do the baking. As I looked at my Attraction Quadrant Sheet (see the model at the end of the chapter), I could more clearly see the negativity that I was continually dumping into my cake mix. No wonder things were a mess—there was nothing wholesome to put frosting on! Perhaps you've been doing the same thing in your life, too. You may find it deeply painful to recognize how upside down your life is. Helping you sort through all of your unconscious patterns is one way an Attraction Quadrant Sheet can be useful. To be successful, you must commit to using it.

Once all the items were categorized, they did not seem so threatening. Maybe, I reasoned, I could work on one item at a time in each category. I understood that in order to change for the better, I needed to identify each of my negative behaviors and *set an intention* to replace it with a positive action. Setting intentions is a powerful practice. www.Princeton.edu defines intention as "an anticipated outcome that is intended or that guides your planned actions."[1] So, what this means to me is that intentions put the energy into deliberately attracting what you want in your life. This is my description of the intention process:

By setting a clear intention, you have the power of your soul behind it.

How do you know this is happening?

You feel a force moving within you. Through your intentions you out-shine self-limiting beliefs and behaviors. Your path becomes clear. Your action steps become intuitive and move you towards your desire. Your energy goes out to and from the Universe deliberately creating your experience. You know the 'force' is with you! You become who you were meant to be!

By identifying what I no longer wanted to feel or to do, I was able to develop a list of intentions for what I wanted to attract into my life. As I concentrated on my intentions for changing my life, the possibilities began to look so much more desirable and manageable. I felt more optimistic and motivated to make changes, and I began to see a path I could follow, one step at a time, to accomplish infinite possibilities. I want to emphasize to you that this took an enormous amount of time, energy, commitment, and focus… it didn't happen overnight. But I realized early in the process that if I did this personal work, I truly had the potential to create a life I loved. The way I set intentions on my Attraction Quadrant Sheet was to focus on and feel the pain of each item that was attacking the quality of my life. Then in my mind's eye I created a picture of what would be an optimal opposite solution for each. Here are some examples:

Painful Negative	Intention
Drinking uncontrollably	Sobriety
Low self-esteem	Self-confidence
Unsatisfying dysfunctional relationships	Relationships based upon accountability and honesty

By writing everything down on my Attraction Quadrant Sheet, I actually found a way to stop meaningless relationships, maintain sobriety, and focus on my real estate business. I had a plan to follow with specific steps to take me into my new life. By identifying my negative events, such as failed relationships, divorce, and self-disdain, I began to reconstruct my life with a list of intentions for each one.

Helen Keller said, "The only thing worse than being blind is having sight and no vision."[3] For the first time ever, I began to have a vision of how I wanted to live: to be free from the chains of alcohol and to wake up each day feeling excited, joyful, and at peace with myself. I was ready to partake in mature and balanced relationships. I could see where I wanted to go and how I wanted to be. The real me— the caring, sensitive, loving, and deeply committed person I knew I was—was ready to emerge from the disguise that alcohol had forced upon me. No longer addicted to my own pain and suffering, I began to live in the satisfying present moment.

Prioritizing the items on my list and working on setting positive intentions gave me an emotional barometer with which I could gauge and then *shift* my emotions. If I felt fearful, angry, depressed, anxious, or resentful, I focused on my planned actions, struggled to put my desires on paper, and pushed myself to make a clear picture of what I wanted to attract to replace those feelings. It took a conscious effort and gut-wrenching commitment. This was the method I used to shift my emotions. My mind-set changed my negative emotions and my feelings became more positive. These transformed emotions then released a powerful energy into the universe, resulting in a new and more desirable vibration surrounding me.

Through my reading and healing work, I learned that the universe is comprised of energy fields. Everything— including your body, thoughts, and emotions—has a vibration. Your vibration is the energy that surrounds you according to the thoughts and feelings you have. As I became more fulfilled, hopeful, and joyful, my vibration was attracting more goodness and well-being into my life. And the stronger the energy became within me, the more items I completed on my list of planned actions. Always reaching for something that felt a little better moved me up the emotional scale. The Law of Attraction states that your vibrational energy attracts a corresponding quality of energy into your life.

I began to update my Attraction Quadrant Sheet weekly, adding more items as I felt better. After working with it for several months, it became a sort of a game. Before long, I was telling myself, *I did that. I accomplished that. So now let's do this.* A perfect example was my drinking. Let me just add, sobriety does not come easily. At first I wanted to stop for a day, and then it went to a week, a month, several months, a year, and so on. I also went from learning to be completely content by myself to attracting new friendships. I kept raising the bar on my desires. You, too, can accomplish exactly what I did. My skills are no different from yours. It was my determination that helped me create a new life for myself.

Here are some examples of what happened in my life as my intention columns expanded. In the area of my work, I wanted to make more of a commitment to my real estate business. As I described at the end of Part One, my intention was to improve my real estate knowledge so as to provide better service to my clients. I started by obtaining different designations through extensive educational training. Each program resulted in an increased level of service and guidance for my clients, smoother transactions for my buyers and sellers, and skills that were instrumental in helping me to open my own business. Eventually, I had so many specialized designations I could not fit them all on my business card. Ultimately, as a result of my intentions, I owned my own multi-million-dollar real estate company.

In the area of my appearance and self-care, I began to follow a disciplined exercise regime. I decided that working with a personal trainer would be helpful and made a commitment to do that. Because I had set this intention, I earned the money to pay for the trainer. Gradually, I lost all the puffiness in my face and built muscle mass in my body. I looked better and felt better as well.

My intentions continued to make my dreams come true. I built the house I had always wanted; found my Jack Russell terrier, Harley, the dog I had envisioned; and married Michael, my fairy-tale prince. I've already told you about finding Harley and how I met Michael, so now I'd like to share with you the story of how I built my house.

In 1985, when I got divorced and started in real estate, I found a beautiful setting for a home, behind a stone wall and facing the reservoir in Framingham. The place was called Stonegate, and the land had been part of a doctor's estate. I drove in through the stone wall onto the private driveway and thought I was in a dream because the setting was so lovely. There were already two buildings that looked like carriage houses and open land for additional new homes that could look out on the water. I began to cry, thinking, *I just got divorced and I will never have the money to live here. How am I ever going to do this? I'm starting all over from scratch. I will never be able to live in a place like this.* Nevertheless, while I was there, I picked up a builder's brochure describing homes that could be built on the property—the houses cost $1 million! (I still have that brochure.)

While I was learning the real estate business, the land went to auction several times, was bought and sold by developers, and then was bought back by the original owner, who didn't want to lose his investment. I continued to develop my business and drove by Stonegate countless times in the next few years as I was showing properties to clients. Always in the back of mind was the hope that I could find a way to live there.

In 1989, I found a picture and architectural plans for a house I loved in a magazine of homes for the Southwest. I put that picture on my bulletin board at work and set an intention for an exquisite new home for myself that would be built to my specifications. I shifted my emotions from despair to hope, and came to believe that my intention would be manifested in reality. Finally, in 1991, six years after initially seeing Stonegate and falling in love with it, I had enough money to buy my dream lot from the original owner of the property. I made an offer and he accepted it! Next, I found a well-respected and talented builder, and hired him to build the house I had envisioned on that lot.

I had never taken on a construction project of this size on my own before. Managing it was a huge job, but it all worked out beautifully. My lovely home has Palladian windows—large, arched windows with three elegantly proportioned segments—that look out on the water. It was the first home in the area to have these windows, and people driving by often stopped to admire them. I have been incredibly happy in my "dream house" with my "dream husband," Michael, and, until the spring of 2010, my little "dream dog," Harley. I have experienced the Law of Attraction at work firsthand.

My Attraction Quadrant Sheet was my recipe for improving my life—I was beginning to bake a delicious cake. I was feeling so much better on the inside, and that was changing my circumstances on the outside. Because the Attraction Quadrant Sheet worked so well for me, I suggest you use it, too. It is a practical tool that will help you identify the problem areas in your life in very precise ways. Putting yourself in alignment with your desires attracts those things into your life.

So now, having begun the ongoing work on Steps 1 and 2, what will you do with this new positive attitude that you've been working on? How will you deal with all this negative stuff? Where will you go from here?

Your Step 3 work is to first identify, as honestly and completely as you can, the areas of turmoil and unhappiness in your life, then to write all of them down in each of the four categories described earlier. Next, you'll need to spend some time imagining with what you want to replace those problems. With perseverance, you will find yourself able to identify exactly what you want your life to look like in every area. Write down your desires as *intentions* opposite each problem situation or negative feeling. By doing this, you will have set your intentions, which begins the process that eventually results in the manifestation of those goals.

Keep your Attraction Quadrant Sheet handy. Whenever you feel upset and challenged by any area of your life, reread the intentions you have set to improve it. Reminding yourself in this way will shift your mind toward more positive thoughts and help generate the energy that will bring your intentions about. Continue to update your Attraction Quadrant Sheet whenever you want to bring more joy into your life through new accomplishments and personal growth.

Preparing and working on my Attraction Quadrant Sheet helped me to think about my life in an entirely new way. Now I know life is meant to be joyful and rewarding, and I know that I have the ability within me to manifest what I can envision. As I write this, I can honestly say that since I started utilizing these steps, I have achieved and acquired so many of my heart's desires.

So take some time to create your own Attraction Quadrant Sheet, identify your negative patterns, and set your intentions for what you want instead. Focus on your planned actions. Keep reaching for something that feels a little better, then something even better than that. The energy around you will put you in alignment with your desires. If you take this process seriously, you will experience proportional results. As your intentions are realized, your life will change in glorious ways. You will learn how to attract fulfillment and joy into your existence. Be assured that good things will happen to you, and know that it will be because *you* will have introduced them into your life.

Action Guide Exercise: Step #3

1 Go to your Attraction Quadrant in the Alpha Chick Action Guide and print out several copies. (Page 7)

2 Identify the top three things you want to change in each quadrant. (Page 6)

3 Set three new intentions in each quadrant that will replace the negative behaviors. (Page 6)

If you don't have your guide yet, please go to:
www. AlphaChick.com/actionguide

Attraction Quadrant Sheet

Mental/Emotional

Problem	Intention
Addiction to alcohol	Sobriety
Feelings of failure	Self-confidence
Poor self-image	Self-love
Poor choices	Feel in control of my life
Trust issues in relationships	Let go of the past
Divorce	Feel free from past mistakes
Fear of rejection	Have trusting, loving relationshi

Spiritual

Lacking beliefs	Spiritual connection
No spiritual practice	Daily meditation/prayer

Physical

Drinking	Sobriety
Poor eating habits	Proper diet
Migraines/frequent colds	Feel healthy consistently
Bad fingernails	Stop picking and chewing

Financial/Career

Not saving money	Save money I spent drinking
No financial reserve	Put 20% of earnings away
No future goals for work	Establish better home life for myse
or lifestyle	Work commitment

Action Steps
Attend AA meetings.
Accomplish one positive thing daily.
Hug myself and daily affirmations.
Focus on what would feel better.
Shift my thinking to the present.
Concentrate on positive aspects.
Establish healthy communications.

Reading and meditation
Get up thirty minutes earlier.
Evening prayers
Set up special space for spiritual practice.
Light special candle for meditation time.

Work the AA twelve steps.
Use previous drinking times for grocery shopping
and cooking.
Proper rest, diet, and vitamins
Physical checkup
Exercise
Weekly manicures

Work with financial planner.
Debt reduction, stop careless shopping
Visualization of a perfect new home
Acquire designations
Become proficient in and better utilize technology.

Step 4:
Thoughts

"Change your thoughts and you change your world."

~ Norman Vincent Peale

For most of my life, I never realized the enormous impact my thoughts had on me. My mind danced constantly between painful memories and the "if onlys" of the future. It seemed to me that my happiness and well-being were dependent upon someone or something in the future, and were never in my control. I had never lived in the present moment until I began to pay attention to my rambling thoughts and do something about them. As I touched on in Part One, when I became consciously aware of my mind's negative "ego voice," I practiced making a positive mental shift (my personal PMS!), which is one of the greatest things you can do for yourself.

Emotions are mostly reactions to your *thinking*. When I am consumed by fear, resentment, or anger, I now know it is because of how I am viewing a particular situation. Invariably, my attention has been on something that has already happened or something that I am dreading will happen. You can recognize negative thoughts about these past or future projections because, when you have them, you will not like how you are feeling at the moment. When I became capable of shifting my thoughts, the unhappiness that had surrounded me for so long began to dissipate. More than anything else, changing your thoughts is instrumental in rebuilding your life and turning your dreams into reality.

Negative thinking causes unhappiness. To put it simply, you are feeling badly because you are thinking badly. But remember, you have the power and the ability to decide how anybody or anything will affect you. Step 4 is an affirmative statement of your control:

I shift my thoughts to the present when I revert to past negative thoughts and feelings.

While you are capable of controlling your thoughts, it requires a conscious effort. Occasionally, I have negative thoughts that come through my ego voice, for which I even have a name—I call her Louise. I think of Louise as my "mini-me." If I let her take over, she can really push me into a downward spiral. Louise believes she is never wrong, and is she ever judgmental! As soon as I hear her sharp, negative voice, I know I need to shift my thinking.

Louise behaves consistently. For instance, when a lack of communication occurs with a friend or a client does not respond as discussed, Louise puts her hands on her hips, taps her toe, and beats me down with her criticism: *They are probably talking to another realtor; why would they want to work with you? You know they will probably never call you. You'd better hold on to every penny you make—you are going to need it.* She goes on and on. I have to pretend her chatter is like a radio, and turn the dial. I have become able to step back, observe, and identify the negative dialogue that takes place in my head. When I identify "Louise talk," I am also able consciously to shift my thoughts to something that feels better and supports the healthy relationships I have with clients and friends. An example is to focus instead on the continued loyalty I have experienced from so many clients during the past twenty-four years.

Early in my recovery from alcoholism, someone suggested that I wear an elastic band on my wrist, which I could pull and release to stop negative thinking. That's because for an alcoholic, such thoughts are associated with the desire to pick up a drink. In Alcoholics Anonymous, they call this desire or conditioning "stinking thinking." The painful snap was like a slap on the wrist, warning me that I was headed into a self-destructive territory and had better stop right away. This was one way of reprogramming myself, and it worked. I recommend that you try this or any other similar little trick that will help remind you to shift your thinking—nothing is too silly if it works. As an Alpha Chick, you will pride yourself on learning to practice useful techniques to help yourself grow and change.

I want to share with you the specific thought-changing technique I learned that you can use together with the elastic band to replace negative thoughts with positive ones. The following actions are taken together and repeated as often as necessary during the day:

- I question, *Why am I feeling this way? What is going on inside of me?*
- I review what has happened in the last twenty-four hours and see what may have caused this thinking.
- I determine whether these thoughts relate to a past event or to something I fear in the future.
- I identify specific thoughts about this situation that would result in my feeling better.
- I repeat these new thoughts to myself several times during the day for reinforcement.

Practicing this thought-changing technique has shown me a way to turn a bad day into a good one and to diffuse negative thought patterns before they get out of control.

Although I may continue to struggle with what is going on in my mind because of all the years that I spent attached to my negative thinking, making the positive mental shift has become the foundation for my survival and fulfillment as an Alpha Chick. I believe it can work for you, too.

Over the years, I have practiced powerful and pleasant activities that create a positive mental shift for me and restore my well-being each day. They are described in the following paragraphs. I suggest you try each one of them to see if they will work for you, especially the first, which for me has been the most effective.

Meditation

My morning meditation practice, in which I listen to and connect with my soul, is the foundation of my day. I have become diligent about meditating every morning, and I get up at 6:30 to allow myself an hour for this. You can start with ten minutes and work your way up to whatever period of time feels right for you. No matter what is happening currently in my life, my meditation experience is calming and reassuring. Sitting in my favorite chair, I light a candle, at times listen to a meditation CD, and settle my mind. Usually it is hard for me to maintain a crazy, racing, and fearful state of being while listening to Gregorian chants or Tibetan bells. I am able to reach a deep connection with my inner essence, or my higher self, and the ego voice becomes silent. Directly following my meditation, I usually write down any ideas that have come to me. They are frequently very powerful insights.

Motivational Material

Every day I read or listen to at least part of a motivational or spiritual book or magazine. These sources give me many inspiring, positive ideas I might not come up with on my own. Making a practice of reading motivational material is guaranteed to uplift your thoughts and feelings. It is part of reprogramming your mind. The quality of what you put into your mind has a significant effect on what comes out of it. My favorite inspirational magazine is *Science of Mind*, which has short, uplifting "daily guides to richer living." This monthly publication is based on the spiritual philosophy of Dr. Ernest Holmes.

Visioning

The technique of "visioning" involves making a clear and detailed mental picture of what you want to attract into your life. I collect actual pictures of things I like or dream about and paste them into a notebook, put them on a bulletin board—what I call my Vision Board—or carry them in my briefcase. Having images around you of what you want to bring into your life and repeatedly thinking about them acts as a powerful magnet to draw them into manifestation. What you desire creates thoughts, which release energy, which attracts these things to you.

You can also do a more structured visioning process that is very effective. Quiet your mind in meditation, and then ask yourself the following four questions and see what arises:

1. What is God's highest vision for my life (or for a particular issue in my life)?
2. What do I have to let go of/surrender for the vision to manifest?
3. What must I embrace for the demonstration of the vision?
4. What else does God wish me to know about this vision?

When you are finished, write down what has come to you and put it where you can review it often.

Here are some specific instances in which visioning has worked for me. As I've already shared with you, I carried an exact picture of Harley in my wallet for two years before I found him in 1994 in Yukon, Oklahoma.

Also, in 1989, I found an architectural rendering of a house that I loved and put it on my Vision Board; I built the house in 1992.

One of my favorite examples concerns a car. I had a picture on my vision board of a Mercedes ML330 for months before they came out in 1996. The cars were so popular they were completely sold out and back-ordered for months. The first dealer I went to treated me like a dumb blond and suggested I could pay *over* list price to get one. My response was "Oh, really?" The second dealership I went to wasn't much better, but they told me they would be happy to put my name on the list of people waiting for the car. The third dealer asked me if I would like to drive the car. This was the first time I actually got to sit in one, and it added that wonderful smell and a physical sensation to my visioning. I placed an order with the manager, realizing it might take time. A week later he called me to let me know that another buyer had changed his mind and asked if I would like to take this car. Miraculously, I got one at sticker price just three weeks after placing my order, which was unheard of because of the short supply. I know that my visioning had brought the car to me!

Visioning can also be done with the written word instead of pictures. In 2000, I wrote a very clear and detailed description of the man I wanted to have in my life. It described this person physically, mentally, emotionally, spiritually, and financially. I often went back to the description to tweak it with additional qualities I thought were important. It became so precise that it was like having a color picture in front of me. As I learned more about Michael when we were dating, I realized how similar he was to the description I had written. Indeed, I ended up marrying the man of my vision.

Visioning has been a huge help in my real estate business as well. I visualize clients with whom I would like to work, houses I would like to sell, and buyers I would like to help. I focus on the specific details of all these desires and bring them about in my life.

Share Your Life with an Animal

As busy as my life was when Harley was alive, I took time every day to get on his big red cushion with him and rub his tummy. You cannot be consumed with negative thoughts, fear, and anger for long when petting an animal. They give unconditional love with no strings attached. When Harley looked at me with his big brown eyes, I had no room for any negativity.

If you don't or can't have a pet, you can still have very positive experiences with animals by spending some time at a local animal shelter. There is always a need for people to exercise dogs or spend time with cats that have been living in the wild and need to get used to human companionship. Just by sitting with these cats, your personal vibrations can help them understand that it is safe to be around people.

You can learn a great deal from animals. They don't hold grudges or retain negative thinking for very long. In *A New Earth*, Eckhart Tolle compares the animal mind to the human mind. He talks about two ducks getting into a terrible fight and pecking at one another viciously. Suddenly they both flap their wings and swim away in different directions as if nothing had happened.[1] Wouldn't it be wonderful, in the midst of a conflict with someone, to just flap your wings and swim away as if there had never been a problem?

Walk Around and Look at Your World

Go outside for a brisk walk. Even a walk in the city can be a nature walk when you look at the trees and flowers. Or look at the faces of the people who pass by—you'll see beauty there, too. When you take time to look at the roses, guess what? You can really smell them! If you have access to a camera, take some photos of things that attract your attention. Pictures you take on your walks will remind you of how much beauty and wonder there is in your world.

Play Games with Small Children

When you play a structured game or create a fantasy game with young kids, making it up as you go along, you will discover that your inner child will come bursting out. Children have no limits to their imagination. They are so free to express themselves, as their minds are not filled with any of the self-criticism or judgments of others we experience as adults. This can rub off on you and activate your own creativity.

Go to a Movie Alone

I love going to a chick flick alone—I can cry or laugh depending on how I feel and not worry about what a companion might think of my response. You can be alone in a movie theater without really feeling alone because other people are nearby. See how this feels to you; you may find it a real treat.

Dance

Dancing is where I really let my emotions fly. I have to admit I am a disco queen and still addicted to the songs of the 1970s. I could play Patti Labelle's *New Attitude* a thousand times and not get tired of it—this is my best feel-good song of all times. You can dance around the house by yourself or invite a friend and dance together. Either way, it'll drive those negative thoughts and images right out of your head!

Take a "Recovery Run"

Instead of exercise, sometimes I will do a quick run through the local Target store. I give myself permission to spend up to $25 on this instant fix, but even a $5 or

$10 limit can be a lot of fun. Set whatever limit works for you, being careful not to engage in this activity more often than you can afford. I get so much stuff— cosmetics, T-shirts, accessories—for under $25, that I end up with a bag full of goodies. You might find Hot Tamale nail polish, deep purple eyeliner, and a fabulous belt covered with silver studs, or some pretty new kitchen towels, a candle, or a silk plant. It's hard to be in a distressed state of mind when you're waltzing through Target finding little goodies to take home and enjoy or give to a friend!

Please know that the Recovery Run is very different from compulsive shopping, which can be just as much of an addiction as alcohol or drugs. It's not a cure for depression or an effort to fill up any kind of an emotional void. Rather, the Recovery Run is a way of treating yourself as an Alpha Chick on an occasional basis.

Volunteer

As women, we can get very caught up in ourselves and our relationships, and often what we dwell upon is not anywhere near as significant as we think it is. Remembering that there are people without enough to eat or dying from incurable diseases is a great antidote for self-pity. Giving them some of your time and energy will help you put your own life into proper perspective and feel good about yourself.

Shortly after Holly passed away, I became involved with the organization called Alex's Lemonade Stands. Alex Scott was an eight-year-old girl battling a fatal childhood cancer. Her mission was to raise money for medical research by selling lemonade from her stand. Alex died young, but not before raising millions of dollars with her lemonade stands nationwide. As of the writing of this book, this charity had raised more than $25 million for research.

I opened a lemonade stand to raise money on Alex's behalf in 2004. It was great to see so many people get excited and pitch in to help. This very special opportunity for me to work with Alex's organization was a most rewarding, mind-shifting experience. It completely moved my focus from the pain and sense of loss I was feeling over Holly's death to something really worthwhile that helped others. When you do something selflessly to help someone in need, you may find it helps you just as much, especially in terms of knowing you have done something worthwhile.

Get a Coach

Because I was starting to feel more secure financially, I decided I wanted to get a business/life coach. A wise and awakened soul, Siobhan Murphy, was recommended to me. Siobhan is what is termed a "Prayer Practitioner" of the Science of Mind spiritual philosophy of Dr. Ernest

Holmes, and she also understands the principles of Twelve Step Recovery and is an astute business coach.

I started working with Siobhan in early 2002, and we immediately bonded on many levels. She skillfully guided me in using the Law of Attraction more in my business planning as well as in my personal interactions with people, and she introduced me to the Science of Mind teachings from which I learned so many ways to reframe my thoughts. Siobhan taught me about the "soul" of the selling process, and about a new paradigm of selling based on service and conscious connection. We used many of her business tools as well, especially the "Order Form" and the "Strategic Attraction Plan," for creating exponential growth in my company.

However, more important than all the things Siobhan taught me was the enormous support she provided for my personal development as an owner of a real estate business and as a motivating leader for the people who work with me. Many times I talked to her about writing a book that I would dedicate to Holly, and she always gave me the greatest encouragement. With Siobhan's assistance, I tapped in to another level of personal power and deliberate, focused thinking.

I cannot emphasize enough the rewards you will receive from having a coach. Personally recognizing the impact it had for me, I decided to become a Certified Professional Coach and make myself available to the readers of *Alpha Chick*. I hope to bring you the clarity you need to empower yourself with smart choices and the tools to discover your true purpose.

These are the things I do to put myself in a positive frame of mind, and I invite you to add your own discoveries as an Alpha Chick to this list of practices. You can contact me personally at mal@alphachick.com and tell me about them, and also share them with the Alpha Chick community at AlphaChick.com.

Always remember that your thoughts determine your reality. A Science of Mind precept is "Change your thinking, change your life." How you think about yourself and your life determines the quality of your existence. I have spoken earlier in this book about the Law of Attraction. Understanding how it works was instrumental in my personal mental transformation. I came to realize in a very profound way that what I think about manifests itself in my physical reality. Now I have an incredibly fulfilling life—a loving husband, his three grown children with whom I have close relationships, a rewarding career, abundant success, good health, and two beautiful homes. My wish is that all women find their own personal happiness that expresses their heart's desires.

The purpose of Step 4 is to show you that by learning to control your thoughts, you can and will change your life. You do not need to sabotage your goals with negative thinking for another day. By learning to think loving and self-respecting things about yourself, you become an Alpha Chick.

I love the following quote from Dr. Walter Doyle Staples, an author and an authority on personal empowerment. He describes so perfectly the link that exists between your thinking and your life:

When you change your thinking, you change your beliefs.
When you change your beliefs, you change your expectations.
When you change your expectations, you change your attitude.
When you change your attitude, you change your behavior.
When you change your behavior, you change your performance.
When you change your performance, you change your life.[4]

This sequence shows a simple and transformative method of shifting your thoughts and making changes in your life. It is not complicated; it just takes commitment and desire. You will soon see the difference it makes in your journey to becoming an Alpha Chick.

Action Guide Exercise: Step #4

1 Pick three new activities that will help you change your negative thinking pattern. (Page 8)

2 How frequently are you going to commit to these new activities.

3 What activity is propelling you to an inspiring future? (Page 9)

4 Write three new affirmations in the present tense for yourself daily. (Page 9)

5 Every morning read for ten minutes your personal affirmations.

6 Start a vision folder and add pictures of things you would like to attract into your life. Daily look at your pictures and express gratitude for all you have and all you are now attracting.

7 Go to AlphaChick.com and share with us what you are attracting into your life.

If you don't have your guide yet,
please go to:
www. AlphaChick.com/actionguide

Step 5:
Healing and Helping

"We are healed of a suffering only by experiencing it in full."

~ Marcel Proust

My healing began as I *focused* on and found my spiritual connection with the divine presence within me in Step 1 of the Alpha Chick Process. With Step 2, I *accepted* my past and developed a new attitude about myself. In Step 3, I *identified* all the things I wanted to change in my life and set intentions and planned actions to do so. I made a *positive mental shift* in Step 4 and replaced my negative thinking with self-empowering *thoughts*. All these actions brought me to a glorious place as I realized the magnificent rewards of all my hard work. The dark veil of depression and self-loathing lifted. I shifted from living tied to my past wounds to celebrating my life in the present moment.

I was now experiencing the light of an awakened self-knowledge, meaning that I was more fully in touch with my true inner being, the real Mal. I was seeing the divine presence in myself and in others. All this allowed me to construct my life so that I could do those things that brought me the greatest joy and happiness. But there was still one final thing to do to complete my healing work. It was time for Step 5 of the Alpha Chick Process:

I heal by reaching out and sharing my journey with others, especially those in need.

The only way to get to Step 5 is to build a foundation by doing the previous steps, being sure that you have completed them thoroughly. You will know you have arrived when you feel you have been healed from your past wounds, although the work of setting intentions for new accomplishments and shifting your thoughts to the positive will continue throughout your life. You will experience an energetic shift in your being and a passion for life you may never have thought possible.

What do I mean by *healing*? TheFreeDictionary online defines to heal as "to restore to health or soundness, to set right."[1] When I use the word *healing* in Step 5, I am referring to a mystical process in which the divine presence within you directs your mind, body, and soul in the way you live your daily life. It is built upon the connection you established in Step 1, Focus. Your physical healing may involve freedom from addiction and improved health and fitness. In the Alpha Chick Process, you experience *spiritual* healing, which is a sense of comfort with your choices and a growing faith, and you begin to trust the voice of your divine presence. Your mental and emotional healing is reinforced every time you are able to let go of a thought, emotion, or experience that disturbs you, and with each intention that you set for a more fulfilling life. You know you are healing as you find yourself going through a day with a reflective awareness and an ability to share your enlightenment with others by helping them to heal as well.

In AA they say, "You can't keep it unless you give it away." The more you "give away" what you have found, the stronger the foundation of your own healing becomes. The help you give to others happens in many ways; you will find ways that are right for you.

Much of my own healing process has evolved from focusing largely on myself to helping other women. Throughout my years of sobriety, I have met many women who have suffered from various addictions, failed relationships, bad marriages, and poor self-esteem. Because of my experiences, I was able to grasp how much these women needed to discover their true nature and their inner voice. I knew they were so much more than the feelings that gripped them and the circumstances that caused their pain. I found myself wanting to help them see that their lives were not defined by their disappointments. I wanted to encourage them to find their own source of infinite wisdom and energy and to change perceptions that made them feel like victims. I had experienced this shift in my own thinking, so I began to believe I could share it. In the words of Michael Josephson, head of the Josephson Institute of Ethics, a nonprofit training and consulting organization based in Southern California:

> We're most vulnerable to victimitis when we're under the influence of powerful emotions like fear, insecurity, anger, frustration, grief or depression. These feelings are so powerful we believe our state of mind is inevitable. Our only hope is that they will go away on their own. Yet it's during times of emotional tumult that using our *power* to choose our thoughts and attitudes is most important. We can't make pain go away, but we can refuse to suffer.[2]

I began by telling my story at AA meetings, but it has grown into so much more than that. Over the years, it has come naturally to me to share much of my own story with women I have met in the many different areas of my life—socially, professionally, and spiritually. I have found myself explaining to them how I use the Alpha Chick steps to overcome the same issues they are facing. I continue to do this now, with friends, colleagues, and even new acquaintances. For me this includes giving away many of the books I have read and the tape and CD programs I have listened to that have become part of my Library of Love. Through my sharing, I have discovered that teaching other women how to make empowering choices reinforces my own recovery and healing. The ability to show them how to find the strength buried under their pain and move forward in their lives strengthens my own mental shift and growth as a person.

Another aspect of sharing has extended to my real estate business. I have freely given information about the detailed systems I have developed to serve our seller and buyer clients, as well as innovative Internet marketing concepts I have used to build a multi-million-dollar business. Along the way, as I described in Part One, people and organizations from all over the United States began to seek me out to participate in their conventions and seminars. I am honored by these requests and want to share what I have learned with as many people as I can. Because I believe we live in an abundant universe and that there are enough riches in the world for everyone, I've never been threatened by the success of others. In fact, this sharing has helped me grow my real estate business to an even higher sales volume.

I continue to coach the real estate agents who join my firm, sharing my creative business plans and best marketing ideas with them. Sometimes, after an agent works with my company and learns all about my special systems and strategies for success, that person is inspired to go out on his or her own. At first I would become upset when that happened, but then I saw that this was my ego reacting—I felt hurt and disappointed that they didn't want to stay with my company, seeing it as a kind of rejection. Then I began to understand that they were really complimenting me. These agents thought enough of my business practices to want to learn what I was doing to become successful and then go out on their own and create their own unique, successful businesses.

I've also tried to help women who are less fortunate than I am financially by sharing knowledge and career guidance and, on occasion, providing monetary assistance when I felt called to help in that way. Helping another woman in trouble is one of the most rewarding experiences for me. There is something about giving to a person in need that creates a feeling of gratitude and appreciation for what you have in your own life. Seeing another woman creating success in her life thrills and inspires me.

In 2003 and 2004, I negotiated a significantly large real estate transaction—the sale of an office park—and overall did nearly $50 million in real estate sales, which put me in a position to expand my giving. In 2006, I was invited by a dear friend to attend the We Are Family Foundation charity ball in New York City, at which they were honoring the deceased teen poet, peace advocate, and motivational speaker, Mattie Stepanek, and singer Elton John, who ended up seated at a table next to mine. Elton was being recognized for his humanitarian efforts and work for HIV/AIDS patients. They showed a moving documentary about his dedication to helping those stricken with AIDS, and I was so inspired by his generosity that I started thinking that I would like to do something similar.

A few weeks after the party, I contacted the We Are Family Foundation about the schools for which they raise money. We Are Family was founded and is run by the legendary singer Nile Rodgers, who wrote and recorded the song by the same name. In conjunction with another charitable educational organization, Building with Books, We Are Family raises money to build schools in Africa, in villages where children would otherwise never have an education. The people from Building with Books recruit students whom they send to Africa to assist local village people with the construction.

After learning more about the work of these two organizations, I committed to financing the construction of the Katherine Holly School in the village of Kondjila in Mali, Africa, which was completed in the fall of 2007. The school opened on December 1 with one hundred students in attendance, fifty-three boys and forty-seven girls. The teachers are local people who have been trained in basic reading, writing, and mathematics. As of this writing, I have not yet been to Kondjila to visit the school, as it is in such a remote place, but I hope to someday.

Financing the construction of the school has been one of the greatest opportunities that I have been given in my life. I cannot put into words how rewarding this project has been for me. Building the school was the greatest way for me to honor the memory of my Sweet Pea, my beautiful niece, Holly, who loved children and education, and wanted to be a child advocate. I hope I will be able to build another school as well—there is someone else I would like to honor in this manner who passed away after Holly.

Writing this book has been another inspiring and empowering experience, as sharing my story to help other women reinforces my own healing. Reliving almost twenty-five years of drinking and all that went with it was very draining emotionally. During the process of working on *Alpha Chick*, I experienced significant health challenges, which I find interesting as I reflect upon them now. I feel the book is a spiritual project, helping me to heal on the deepest spiritual levels.

I started writing *Alpha Chick* in the spring of 2008. During that summer, I started to feel slightly ill, and in the fall I had an emergency appendectomy, followed in two weeks by another emergency surgery for a massive infection at the appendectomy incision site. It felt like something was trying to stop me from writing the book. After three CAT scans, the doctors decided I had an enlarged pancreatic duct that required close monitoring. Over the winter, I started to recuperate, only to be stricken with severe viral gastritis in April of 2009, following an endoscopy exam to have a look at my insides. Every time I resumed working on the book, something would impede my progress again. This illness lasted almost six months.

However, I refused to be sidetracked by all of this. No matter what was happening with my personal health, I kept working on the book. This is reminiscent to me of how Holly had continued her schooling goals in the face of her health challenges. It felt like my intention was being challenged, almost tested, all along the way. Astonishingly, the head of internal medicine at the hospital called to tell me that after reviewing the MRI from November of 2009, he'd found that the pancreatic duct was now normal in size and that they had no medical explanation for this reversal. In fact, he had never seen this happen before.

But *I* have an explanation. My unwavering commitment to writing this book gave me all the answers I needed for my healing. As the project drew to completion, I began to feel even more inspired. I used all the tools of the five steps to deal with the physical and mental blocks I was experiencing. Putting my life story on paper has made me realize over and over again how fortunate I am and how far I have come by using the Alpha Chick steps.

I hope that you will be encouraged by my story to do your own work to come to know that you have the ability to heal from your wounds. You can transcend the pain and fear in your life and replace them with healing practices. Healing, learning, and creating are different aspects of the same process. You will find that the greatest gift you will receive from your own healing experience is being able to reach out and help others transcend the pain and suffering that is temporarily blocking access to the creative expression of their souls.

When you are ready for Step 5, take some time to think about areas in which you would feel the most comfortable reaching out to others. Following are a few ideas, and I'm sure you can think of more—something that is just right *for you*.

On a local level, many churches offer women's support groups for various illnesses, divorce, and grief counseling. Participating in such a group would help you grow and give you a safe place to share your own experiences with women who could benefit from knowing what you have overcome.

The American Cancer Society has a program called Reach for Recovery, in which women who have survived breast cancer are paired with others recently diagnosed with this potentially life-threatening disease. If you are a cancer survivor, this program might be just right for you. Volunteering to visit hospitalized or shut-in women is another option, as is helping out at a nursing home, which can be a lonely and isolating place.

Most cities have Big Sister organizations and Girls Clubs. Working with children at a Girls Club is a meaningful way to help girls avoid some of the mistakes you have made by serving as a role model. Get to know these girls and enjoy them. Many of the girls looking for a Big Sister are from broken and addictive homes where they may have experienced physical and emotional abuse. Some may have lost their mothers; all are very needy. It is important to understand, though, that being a Big Sister is a major commitment. The organization conducts background checks, trains participants, and asks them for weekly contact with their Little Sister over a period of at least one year. Give this decision a lot of thought—pray or meditate about it before you go forward. Volunteer work at the Girls Clubs or with a church group would help you become ready to be a Big Sister.

Boston has a well-known women's shelter and rehabilitation program called Rosie's Place, which is designed especially for women by women. I've gone there during the Christmas holiday season to help serve meals. Perhaps there is a "Rosie's Place" in your community. Volunteering at a women's shelter provides insight into your own life as well as support for others who really need it. And don't forget to "bloom where you are planted." Sometimes the people you can help the most are closest to home—your friends, neighbors, classmates, and/or colleagues at work.

A word of caution is probably appropriate at this point. Helping others is something that should gradually be woven into the fabric of your life. You don't need to become a missionary—going up and down the streets looking for women to rescue is not what Step 5 intends. Rather, I want to encourage you to feel comfortable with yourself and know you are living in an expanded consciousness and wisdom. Then look around and see how and where you might be useful. Be low-key about it. Start with small steps, such as offering a kind word, compassion, a smile, a listening ear, a cup of tea, or a quiet place after an argument. Share a book or CD that you have found helpful. As you do these things, your healing will show through to others and your path will be revealed to you.

You will feel truly fulfilled as an Alpha Chick when you are able to help other women overcome their struggles by sharing the example of your own recovery. You will come to understand what an outstretched hand or a comforting hug can do for a scared and unraveled soul. You know all too well what your wounds have felt like and how alone you have felt at times.

As we've discussed, the Alpha Chick Process is designed to create mental, emotional, physical, financial, and spiritual transformation. If you follow these five steps, all areas of your life—career, friends, love, family, and even physical surroundings—will improve in ways that you yourself have attracted and created. You will become the Alpha Chick you were meant to be.

Action Guide Exercise: Step #5

1 What one activity of service to others
   can you add to your list? (Page 10)

2 How do you think this activity will make
   you feel?

3 Identify one person you know personally
   that you can do something for that will
make a difference in their life. (Page 10)

4 List one activity that you feel
   empowers you.

If you don't have your guide yet,
please go to:
www. AlphaChick.com/actionguide

About the Author

Mal Duane has triumphed over devastating life challenges to become an Alpha Chick extraordinaire. Today she serves clients through the multi-million dollar real  estate company that she built from scratch. She has a dream marriage and as a certified Professional Coach is deeply involved with helping women discover and use their connection with the divine power within them to become their own version of an Alpha Chick.

Her life experience, including recovering from a decades-long struggle with alcoholism, has provided her with extensive hands-on, in-the-trenches know-how for taking hold of a life and bringing forward the potential that lies buried beneath the scars and hurts. She generously shares what she has learned at every opportunity.

Mal lives with her husband, Dr. Michael Pearlman (also known as Dr. Delicious), and their English Jack Russell Terrier, Hannah, in Framingham, Massachusetts where she works, writes, speaks, and supports women in being the best they can be.

How to Engage the Author

MAL DUANE, Certified Professional Coach, is available to share her compelling story and her unique Five Steps for Moving from Pain to Power with you as a personal coach or with your organization. Contact Alpha Chick Associates to discuss speaking, coaching or teleseminars. Please visit www.AlphaChick.com for additional information or contact:

Alpha Chick Associates

256 Salem End Road

Framingham, MA 01702

508-416-1800

malduane@alphachick.com

Mal's Library of Love

I am so happy to share with you the current selections in my Library of Love. When I started my journey of recovery, I personally found great comfort in many of the books I read and audio programs to which I listened. I would often suggest these to other women whom I met along the way, and over time people began to ask me what I was reading or recommended. So for many years, I have kept a list of my top twenty-five favorites in each category. The list often changes because of the new books that I read and love. I hope it will be helpful for you, providing selections that you feel may enlighten and aid you in your journey of personal discovery.

Books

Allen, James. *As a Man Thinketh.*

Ban Breathnach, Sarah. *Simple Abundance: A Daybook of Comfort and Joy.*

Beck, Martha. *Finding Your Own North Star: Claiming the Life You Were Meant to Live.*

Butterworth, Eric. *Discover the Power Within You: A Guide to the Unexplored Depths Within.*

Canfield, Jack. *The Success Principles: How to Get from Where You Are to Where You Want to Be.*

Chopra, Deepak. *The Seven Spiritual Laws of Success: A Practical Guide to the Fulfillment of Your Dreams.*

Cruse, Sharon. *Learning To Love Yourself*

Dooley, Mike. *Infinite Possibilities: The Art of Living Your Dreams.*

Dyer, Wayne. *The Shift: Taking Your Life from Ambition to Meaning.*

Fox, Emmett. *Power Through Constructive Thinking.*

Hay, Louise L. *You Can Heal Your Life.*

Hicks, Esther and Jerry. *Ask and It Is Given: Learning to Manifest Your Desires.*

Hill, Napoleon. *Think and Grow Rich.*

Hill, Napoleon. *You Can Work Your Own Miracles.*

Holmes, Ernest. *The Science of Mind.*

Kushner, Harold S. *When Bad Things Happen to Good People.*

Murphy, Joseph. *Maximize Your Potential Through the Power of Your Subconscious Mind to Create Wealth and Success.*

Ponder, Catherine. *The Dynamic Laws of Prosperity.*

Price, John Randolph. *The Workbook for Self-Mastery: A Course of Study on the Divine Reality.*

Richardson, Cheryl. *Life Makeovers: 52 Practical and Inspiring Ways to Improve Your Life One Week at a Time.*

Robinson, Lynn A. *Divine Intuition: Your Guide to Creating a Life You Love.*

Sharma, Robin S. *The Monk Who Sold His Ferrari: A Fable About Fulfilling Your Dreams and Reaching Your Destiny.*

Taylor, Sandra Anne. *Secrets of Success: The Science and Spirit of Real Prosperity.*

Tolle, Eckhart. *The Power of Now: A Guide to Spiritual Enlightenment.*

Wattles, Wallace D. *The Science of Getting Rich or Financial Success Through Creative Thought.*

Yogananda, Paramhansa. *The Wisdom of Yogananda, vol. 4, How to Be a Success.*

Audio/CDs

Ban Breathnach, Sarah. *Simple Abundance: Living by Your Own Lights.*

Beattie, Melody. *Codependent No More: How to Stop Controlling Others and Start Caring for Yourself.*

Beckwith, Michael Bernard. *Life Visioning: A Four-Stage Evolutionary Journey to Live as Divine Love.*

Bristol, Claude. *The Magic of Believing: The Science of Setting Your Goal and Then Reaching It.*

Chopra, Deepak. *Reinventing the Body, Resurrecting the Soul: How to Create a New You.*

Covey, Stephen R. *The 7 Habits of Highly Effective People.*

Dyer, Wayne. *Manifest Your Destiny: The Nine Spiritual Principles for Getting Everything You Want.*

Dyer, Wayne. *The Power of Intention.*

Grabhorn, Lynn. *Excuse Me, Your Life Is Waiting: The Astonishing Power of Feelings.*

Hay, Louise L. *Self-Healing: Loving Affirmations for Achieving and Maintaining Optimum Health.*

Hicks, Esther and Jerry. *Ask and It Is Given, Part 1, The Law of Attraction.*

Hill, Napoleon. *The Science of Personal Achievement.*

Holmes, Ernest. *Live Again! 2: Spiritual Mind Treatment.*

Khechog, Nawang. *Tibetan Meditation Music.*

Orloff, Judith. *Positive Energy: 10 Extraordinary
   Prescriptions for Transforming Fatigue, Stress, and
   Fear into Vibrance, Strength, and Love.*
Peale, Norman Vincent. *The Power of Positive Thinking.*
Robbins, Anthony. *Awaken the Giant Within: How to
   Take Immediate Control of Your Mental, Emotional,
   Physical and Financial Destiny!*
Rohn, Jim. *The Art of Exceptional Living.*
Ruiz, Miguel. *The Four Agreements: A Practical Guide
   to Personal Freedom.*
Shimoff, Marci. *Happy for No Reason: 7 Steps to Being
   Happy from the Inside Out.*
Thompson, Jeffrey. *Brain Wave Suite.*
Tolle, Eckhart. *A New Earth: Awakening to Your Life's
   Purpose.*
Tolle, Eckhart. *Practicing the Power of Now: Essential
   Teachings, Meditations, and Exercises from the Power
   of Now.*
Virtue, Doreen. *Chakra Clearing: Awakening Your
   Spiritual Power to Know and Heal.*
Williamson, Marianne. *A Return to Love: Reflections
   on the Principles of "A Course in Miracles."*

Notes

Mal-function

1. Ernest Hemingway, *A Farewell to Arms* (New York: Charles Scribner & Sons, 1929), 249.

Sweet Pea

1. "Hemophilia: The Royal Disease," Aaron Nazarian and Idan Ivri, accessed August 25, 2010, http://www.knowledgene.com.
2. "President Clinton Signs Ricky Ray Hemophilia Relief Fund Into Law; Community Rejoices," PRNewswire, Friday November 13, 1998, http://www.aegis.com/news/pr/1998/PR981108.html.

Step 1

1. 1 Cor. 13:12 (King James Version).
2. *Alcoholics Anonymous*, 3rd ed. (New York: Alcoholics Anonymous World Services, 1976).
3. Jiddu Krishnamurti, "On God" (lecture, London, October 1949).
4. Eckhart Tolle, *The Power of Now* (Novato, CA: New World Library, 2001), 168–169.
5. Eugene Holden, Daily Guides, "Non-Attachment," *Science of Mind*, August 2009, 54.
6. Matthew 7:7 (New International Version).

Step 2

1. Authorship of this prayer is commonly attributed to the theologian Reinhold Niebuhr (1936).
2. Maya Angelou Quotes, http://brainyquote.com/quotes/quotes/m/mayaangelo101310.html.

Step 3

1. WordNet, s.v. "intention," http://wordnetweb.princeton.edu/perl/webwn?s=intention.
2. Helen Keller, quoted in Daily Guides, "Vision," *Science of Mind*, August 15, 2009, 48.

Step 4

1. Eckhart Tolle, *The Power of Now* (Novato, CA: New World Library, 2001), 156.
2. Walter Doyle Staples, *Think Like a Winner* (Wilshire Book Co. March 1993), 140.
3. Walter Doyle Staples, *Think Like a Winner* (Wilshire Book Co. March 1993).

Step 5

1. The Free Dictionary, s.v. "healing," http://www.thefreedictionary.com/healing.
2. Michael Josephson, "Curing Victimitis," (radio commentary 643.1, October 30, 2009).

CPSIA information can be obtained at www.ICGtesting.com
Printed in the USA
BVOW011831140212

282936BV00001B/4/P

9 780983 412908